KATHY HEDGE

D1603681

ENGAGING
YOUR BOARD IN FUNDRAISING

A STAFF'S GUIDE

BOARDSOURCE®

Library of Congress Cataloging-in-Publication Data

Hedge, Kathy.
    Engaging your board in fundraising : a staff's guide / Kathy Hedge.
        pages cm
    Includes bibliographical references.
    ISBN 1-58686-145-X
    1. Fund raising. 2. Boards of directors. 3. Nonprofit organizations--
Management. I. Title.
    HV41.2.H426 2014
    658.15'224--dc23
                                                        2014003375

© 2014 BoardSource.
ISBN 1-58686-145-X

Published by BoardSource
750 9th Street, NW, Suite 650
Washington, DC 20001

BoardSource is dedicated to advancing the public good by building exceptional nonprofit boards and inspiring board service.

BoardSource was established in 1988 by the Association of Governing Boards of Universities and Colleges (AGB) and Independent Sector (IS). Prior to this, in the early 1980s, the two organizations had conducted a survey and found that although 30 percent of respondents believed they were doing a good job of board education and training, the rest of the respondents reported little, if any, activity in strengthening governance. As a result, AGB and IS proposed the creation of a new organization whose mission would be to increase the effectiveness of nonprofit boards.

With a lead grant from the Kellogg Foundation and funding from five other donors, BoardSource opened its doors in 1988 as the National Center for Nonprofit Boards with a staff of three and an operating budget of $385,000. On January 1, 2002, BoardSource took on its new name and identity. These changes were the culmination of an extensive process of understanding how we were perceived, what our audiences wanted, and how we could best meet the needs of nonprofit organizations.

Today, BoardSource is the premier voice of nonprofit governance. Its highly acclaimed products, programs, and services mobilize boards so that organizations fulfill their missions, achieve their goals, increase their impact, and extend their influence. BoardSource is a 501(c)(3) organization.

BoardSource provides

- resources to nonprofit leaders through workshops, training, and an extensive website (www.boardsource.org)

- governance consultants who work directly with nonprofit leaders to design specialized solutions to meet an organization's needs

- the world's largest, most comprehensive selection of material on nonprofit governance, including a large selection of books and CD-ROMs

- an annual conference that brings together approximately 700 governance experts, board members, and chief executives and senior staff from around the world

For more information, please visit our website at www.boardsource.org, e-mail us at mail@boardsource.org, or call us at 800-883-6262.

Essential Resources from BoardSource

The Governance Series

Ten Basic Responsibilities of Nonprofit Boards, Second Edition
Legal Responsibilities of Nonprofit Boards, Second Edition
Financial Responsibilities of Nonprofit Boards, Second Edition
Fundraising Responsibilities of Nonprofit Boards, Second Edition
The Nonprofit Board's Role in Mission, Planning, and Evaluation, Second Edition
Structures and Practices of Nonprofit Boards, Second Edition

The Committee Series

Transforming Board Structure: Strategies for Committees and Task Forces
Governance Committee
Executive Committee
Financial Committees
Development Committee
Advisory Councils

Other Publications

Better Bylaws: Creating Effective Rules for Your Nonprofit Board, Second Edition

Board Fundamentals: Understanding Roles in Nonprofit Governance, Second Edition

Building the Governance Partnership: The Chief Executive's Guide to Getting the Best from the Board, Second Edition

Chief Executive Succession Planning: Essential Guidance for Boards and CEOs, Second Edition

Chief Executive Transitions: How to Hire and Support a Nonprofit CEO

Culture of Inquiry: Healthy Debate in the Boardroom

Driving Strategic Planning: A Nonprofit Executive's Guide, Second Edition

Fearless Fundraising for Nonprofit Boards, Second Edition

Generate Buzz: Strategic Communication for Nonprofit Boards, Second Edition

Govern Green: Driving Your Organization's Commitment to Sustainability

Govern More, Manage Less: Harnessing the Power of Your Nonprofit Board, Second Edition

Governance as Leadership: Reframing the Work of Nonprofit Boards

Managing Conflicts of Interest: The Board's Guide to Unbiased Decision Making, Third Edition

Meeting, and Exceeding Expectations: A Guide to Successful Nonprofit Board Meetings, Second Edition

Moving Beyond Founder's Syndrome to Nonprofit Success

Navigating the Organizational Lifecycle: A Capacity-Building Guide for Nonprofit Leaders

Nonprofit Executive Compensation: Planning, Performance, and Pay, Second Edition

Taming the Troublesome Board Member

The Board Building Cycle: Nine Steps to Finding, Recruiting, and Engaging Nonprofit Board Members, Second Edition

The Board Chair Handbook, Third Edition

The Business Professional's Guide to Nonprofit Board Service: Leveraging Your Talents for the Social Sector, Second Edition

The Handbook of Nonprofit Governance

The Nonprofit Board Answer Book: A Practical Guide for Board Members and Chief Executives, Third Edition

The Nonprofit Chief Executive's Ten Basic Responsibilities, Second Edition

The Nonprofit Dashboard: Using Metrics to Drive Mission Success, Second Edition

The Source: Twelve Principles of Governance That Power Exceptional Boards

Trouble at the Top: The Nonprofit Board's Guide to Managing an Imperfect Chief Executive

Understanding Nonprofit Financial Statements, Third Edition

Who's Minding the Money? An Investment Guide for Nonprofit Board Members, Second Edition

Wrestling with Board Dilemmas: Case Studies for Nonprofit Leaders

Toolkits
Assessing and Supporting Your Chief Executive
Boardroom Chemistry: Getting Your Board to Govern as a Team
Diversity in Action
Fearless Filing: Conquering Form 990's Governance Questions
Fundraising Fitness
Getting On Board with Effective Orientation
New Voices at the Table
Recruiting a Stronger Board
Strategic Planning: Understanding the Process

Assessments
Board Self-Assessment
Assessment of the Chief Executive
Executive Search — Needs Assessment
Peer-to-Peer Assessment
Diversity & Inclusion Assessment

For information and prices on publications, assessments, consulting, training, and membership, please visit www.boardsource.org.

FOREWORD

The challenges that organizations face in securing the resources they need to succeed are well documented. Many organizations are teetering on the edge of failure, and many more are forced to forgo advances in their programs or services due to a lack of resources.

At BoardSource, we often hear the frustration and angst from chief executives who are facing these tough realities. Said one chief executive participating in the 2010 *BoardSource Nonprofit Governance Index*, "I am so busy writing grants and trying to raise the money to pay the mortgage and keep the doors open that I don't have time to get out and develop relationships, cultivate donors, etc. The board has got to become more involved and committed to its fiscal responsibility."

This connection between executive angst around fundraising results and frustration with board fundraising performance is real. According to a 2013 report from CompassPoint and the Evelyn & Walter Haas, Jr. Fund, *Underdeveloped: A National Study of Challenges Facing Nonprofit Fundraising,* 75 percent of all executives say that board member engagement in fundraising is "insufficient," with 17 percent of executives indicating that their boards have no involvement in fundraising at all.

BoardSource's 2012 *Nonprofit Governance Index* indicated that fundraising is the lowest ranked area of board performance, with only 5 percent of all chief executives assigning their boards an "A" and 75 percent giving their boards a "C" or below. And, underscoring the frustration around board participation in fundraising, 40 percent of CEOs report that their boards "rely mostly on the CEO and staff" to fundraise, despite the fact that 75 percent of CEOs report that "expectations related to fundraising are clearly explained during recruitment."

But it's not just boards that are shouldering the blame when fundraising results are lackluster. According to *UnderDeveloped*, roughly a third of all executive directors are "lukewarm or dissatisfied" with the performance of their development directors. And, conversely, less than half of all development directors say that they have a strong fundraising partnership with the executive director, with 21 percent of all development directors characterizing the partnership as "weak" or "nonexistent."

The frustration between boards, executives, and development directors is understandable. If you're not getting the results that your organization needs, then it's reasonable to ask the question about whether or not you have the right people on board to deliver those results. But boards, executives, and development staff all too often get stuck in a blame game focused on determining whose responsibility it is to fundraise, instead of tackling the core issues that might enable them to achieve stronger results.

To move beyond blame requires courage and commitment, and a willingness on someone's part to take the first step. This book suggests that the staff has the opportunity — if not the responsibility — to take the lead. And it provides practical advice on how to take the first step, and the many steps after that.

It is our hope that this book — and the conversations that emerge around it — can provide a pathway out of the blame game toward a stronger, more productive fundraising partnership between your board and staff. One that unleashes the full fundraising potential of the board in a positive and affirming way, and that propels your organization forward in ways that are powerful and real.

Anne Wallestad
President & CEO
BoardSource

ACKNOWLEDGMENTS

The idea for this book first surfaced a few years ago when an acquaintance of mine, who was an executive director for a small nonprofit, lamented that her board was not more involved in fundraising. She said to me, "I wish my board would be more involved in fundraising so that I won't have to be!" I found the comment surprising. Having worked with board members and fundraising for over 20 years myself, my immediate thought was, "If you are able to successfully involve your board members in fundraising, you will have more work to do, not less!"

From that time on, the idea for this book has been percolating. In the pages that follow, you will find a framework that focuses on the *staff's role* in engaging your board in fundraising. It's based on my own experience and the insights of nearly 50 nonprofit practitioners and professionals, along with learnings from motivation research that I have applied to the fundraising area. And the results show reason for encouragement: Board member engagement in fundraising is NOT out of our hands — we as staff *can* make a difference!

I would like to thank the numerous individuals who made this book possible. First, my deep thanks to the terrific BoardSource team that saw the value of this topic, steered this project, and provided editorial review: Anne Wallestad, Rita Santelli, Danielle M. Henry, Anne Atwood Mead, and Outi Flynn. I would also like to thank everyone who provided input on content, editorial review, and recommendations for interview candidates: Marla Bobowick, Colleen Campbell Bozard, Elizabeth Costas, Ginna Goodenow, Karen Green, James Greenfield, Lea Harvey, Debbie Hechinger, Mark Hierholzer, Kathleen Rae King, Chuck Loring, Marci Bernstein Lu, Anne Maynard, Josh Mintz, Paula Morris, Rick Moyers, Char Mollison, Jane O'Connell, Julie Price, Susan Price, Maegan Scott, Robert Shalett, Paula Shoecraft, Larry Slesinger, Dave Sternberg, Don Tebbe, and Linda Wood. And a very special thanks to Kathleen Rae King for encouraging me to write this book in the first place, and my husband Russ for encouraging and assisting me along the way.

This book reflects the learnings and experience of the nearly 50 nonprofit leaders I interviewed. I am deeply grateful to all of them for sharing their insights with me as staff members, board members, consultants, and/or funders of nonprofits. Throughout the book you will see numerous examples, quotes, and stories from those interviewed. They make the advice in this book come to life.

My deep gratitude goes to all of those interviewed:

Hedrick Belin, President, Potomac Conservancy, Silver Spring, MD

Charlotte Berry, Board Member, United Way Association of South Carolina; Founding Member, Women in Philanthropy; former National Chairperson, Volunteers for the American Red Cross, Columbia, SC

Nicole Marie Boisvert, Director of External Relations, Good Shepherd Services, New York, NY

Lisa Brandeburg, Vice President, Communications and Development, Volunteers of America of North Louisiana, Shreveport, LA

Jim Cason, Associate Executive Secretary for Strategic Advocacy, Friends Committee on National Legislation, Washington, DC

Patricia Cornell, Director of Development, Food & Friends, Washington, DC

Elizabeth Costas, Executive Director, The Frances L. & Edwin L. Cummings Memorial Fund, New York, NY

Jen Cox, Director of Development, Taxpayers for Common Sense, Washington, DC

Matthew Downey, Program Director, Nonprofit Services, Johnson Center for Philanthropy, Grand Valley State University, Grand Rapids, MI

Jessica Favret, Director of Development, Cristo Rey Jesuit High School, Baltimore, MD

Betsy Garside, Managing Director, Garside Group, Washington, DC

Sara Gibson, Chief Development and Communications Officer, Miriam's Kitchen, Washington, DC

James M. Greenfield, Author and Fundraising Consultant, J.M. Greenfield & Associates, Lacey, WA

Lea Harvey, Vice President of Development, Resources for the Future, Washington, DC

Debbie Hechinger, Consultant, Jackson Hole, WY; Board Member, Grand Teton National Park Foundation, Jackson, WY; BoardSource Senior Governance Consultant

Mark Hierholzer, Consultant, Hierholzer Consulting, Richmond, VA

Jennifer Hoffman, Deputy Director, Prince George's Child Resource Center, Largo, MD

Kathleen Rae King, former National Vice President for Development, Volunteers of America, Alexandria, VA

Sr. Paulette LoMonaco, Executive Director, Good Shepherd Services, New York, NY

Chuck Loring, Senior Partner, Loring, Sterling & Associates, Ft. Lauderdale, FL; BoardSource Senior Governance Consultant

Leslie Mattson, President, Grand Teton National Park Foundation, Jackson, WY

Daniel McQuaid, President & CEO, One OC (formerly Volunteer Center Orange County), Santa Ana, CA

Layli Miller-Muro, Executive Director, Tahirih Justice Center, Falls Church, VA

Amelia Montjoy, Vice President, Resource Development, Ocean Conservancy, Washington, DC

Paula Morris, Program Director, Flexible Leadership Awards Program, A Project of the Tides Center and the Evelyn & Walter Haas, Jr. Fund, San Francisco, CA

Amy Nakamoto, Executive Director, DC SCORES, Washington, DC

August Napoli, Jr., Deputy Director and Chief Advancement Officer, Cleveland Museum of Art, Cleveland, OH

Denise Nelson, Vice President, Resource Development, PENCIL, New York, NY

Jane O'Connell, President, Altman Foundation, New York, NY; Trustee and Treasurer, Museum of the City of New York; Board Member, VCG/Governance Matters.

Heather Reynolds, President/CEO, Catholic Charities Ft. Worth, Ft. Worth, TX

Steve Richards, Board Chair, Sustainable Harvest International; Principal, Strategic Fundraising, Mount Desert, ME

Patrick Rooney, Associate Dean for Academic Affairs and Research, Indiana University Lilly Family School of Philanthropy, Indianapolis, IN

David Rubenstein, Principal, Thoughtful Action Group, Washington, DC

Scott Schenkelberg, President & CEO, Miriam's Kitchen, Washington, DC

Craig Shniderman, Executive Director, Food & Friends, Washington, DC

Sharon Spira-Cushnir, Chief Operating Officer, St. Anne's, Los Angeles, CA; former President & Chief Executive Officer, Executive Service Corps of Southern California, Los Angeles, CA

Ken Strmiska, Vice President for Advancement, Strategy, and Innovation, Lakeland College, Sheboygan, WI

David Livington Styers, Director, Consulting Services, Center for Volunteer and Nonprofit Leadership, San Rafael, CA; BoardSource Senior Governance Consultant

Joseph T.N. Suarez, CFRE, Executive Advisor, Community Partnerships, Booz Allen Hamilton, Rockville, MD

Rev. John W. Swope, S.J., President, Cristo Rey Jesuit High School, Baltimore, MD

Kelly Updike, Executive Director, Embassy Theatre, Ft. Wayne, IN

Nancy Wackstein, Executive Director, United Neighborhood Houses, New York, NY

Carol Weisman, President, Board Builders, St. Louis, MO; Board President, Friends of the Children's Eternal Rainforest, Costa Rica; Board Member, Trailnet, St. Louis, MO

John Westfall-Kwong, Director of Development, Lambda Legal, New York, NY

E. Carlton "Buddy" Wilton, Jr., Philanthropist and Board Member (multiple organizations), Ketchum, ID

Marti Worshtil, Executive Director, Prince George's Child Resource Center, Largo, MD

Ilir Zherka, Executive Director, National Conference on Citizenship, Washington, DC

Jessica Ziegler, Director of Development, United Neighborhood Houses, New York, NY

INTRODUCTION:
FRAMING THE PROBLEM

Read This Chapter First!

"I can't get my board to fundraise!" If you've thought that lately, then this book is for you!

And you are not alone. Studies show that board member participation in fundraising is considered to be inadequate by executive directors and board members alike (see sidebar at right).

When seeking solutions to address this issue, many fundraisers start by asking the question, "What are the barriers that keep board members away from fundraising?" Certainly this is a very good question to ask. Some board members do not feel comfortable asking their friends or colleagues for a financial contribution to their organization, or they may worry about reciprocity. Others have mistaken notions of fundraising; they see it as "cold-calling" or "arm-twisting," and only about "asking for money."

While it's helpful to examine the barriers for board members, I suggest that it's not the only question to ask. It's equally important to look at what is keeping *staff members* from being more successful at engaging board members in fundraising. Of course, the end result is still the same — board members more motivated and ready to raise funds to advance our

SPOTLIGHT ON FINDINGS
Surveys Show Lackluster Board Engagement in Fundraising

Recent studies show that involving board members in fundraising continues to be a challenge for many nonprofits. In the 2012 *BoardSource Nonprofit Governance Index,* a substantial number of chief executives — 40 percent — reported that their board members are reluctant to participate in fundraising. In addition, 'fundraising' was the lowest scoring area of performance among the board's basic responsibilities — a ranking that has been constant in the 20 years of the survey.

In the study, *UnderDeveloped: A National Study of Challenges Facing Nonprofit Fundraising,* released in 2013, 75 percent of executive directors called board engagement in fundraising "insufficient" and 17 percent reported no board involvement in fundraising at all.

Even board members rate their fundraising performance to be lackluster. In research conducted for her 2012 book, *Donor Centered Leadership,* Penelope Burk found that board members gave themselves collectively a 4.7 on a 7-point scale to this statement: "My board makes a significant contribution to the bottom line through fundraising" (on the 7-point scale, a score of 5.2 or higher was considered marginally effective; a score of 5.7 was considered very effective).

missions. But the path to success depends to a large extent on the *staff members* who support, guide, and engage the board.

Make no mistake — participation in fundraising is part of a board's core responsibility of ensuring adequate resources to advance the organization's mission. But it is the staff's responsibility to inform, engage, train, facilitate, and support board members in undertaking activities that will advance the fundraising program on behalf of the nonprofit. With our in-depth knowledge of the organization and fundraising, we are best positioned to create an encouraging environment that supports board member involvement.

So what are the barriers that keep us as staff from being more successful in engaging board members to fundraise? And how can we increase our chances for success?

HOW ARE WE MISSING THE MARK?

The executive directors and development directors interviewed for this book identified a number of reasons why we as staff sometimes miss the mark when it comes to engaging our board members in fundraising. Perhaps you will relate with one or more of the sentiments below:

- **We forget that board members are volunteers.** Board members have busy lives — most have professional jobs, families, and other civic and volunteer obligations. They do not live in the day-to-day reality of our nonprofit organizations the way we do. When we forget this, we don't provide adequate context and background on issues, and we don't reinforce the connection to the mission that board members need on a regular basis to keep them engaged and motivated. Staff also overestimates what board members know about their organizations, and we underestimate how much support and assistance board members need to be successful in fundraising.

- **We are waiting for board members to mobilize themselves and take the initiative around fundraising.** Most board members don't join the board with the express purpose of fundraising. And board members who are uncomfortable with the notion of fundraising are unlikely to step up on their own. More importantly, in most organizations with professional staff, fundraising is a *staff-led* function that board members assist with, so board members depend on us to mobilize them and give them guidance — respectfully and with a deft touch.

- **We don't set clear expectations about fundraising with individuals before they join the board.** Some nonprofit leaders are reluctant, even nervous, about having the "fundraising conversation" with a prospective board member, so they gloss over the topic instead of being crystal clear about expectations. Other times, the conversation centers around the personal giving of board members with little to no attention paid to how board members are expected to be involved in the rest of the fundraising process. When we do talk about the fundraising process, we keep it vague by simply saying, "board members are expected to assist with fundraising," without explaining what that means.

- **We start the conversation about fundraising at the wrong place and at the wrong time.** We often introduce the topic of fundraising to our board by announcing a training session for board members, or by setting out how we expect them to play a role in the annual campaign. From the board member's perspective, this is not the way or place to begin. Rather, we need to explain the need, provide context, clarify roles, and build consensus so that there is a common understanding about why the organization is reaching out to the board around fundraising at this time.

- **We use a "one-size-fits-all" approach.** Not all board members can or will engage in fundraising activities in the same way. Some board members may turn out to be fantastic solicitors of gifts, but some will be better deployed in activities that do not involve asking. And if your board has traditionally not been very engaged in fundraising, the process of getting them involved may take some time. Staff members who rely on a "one-size-fits-all" approach, and who expect board engagement to be a relatively quick process, are likely to become frustrated and will frustrate board members as well.

- **We don't know how to "manage up."** Supporting and managing board member participation requires the tricky skill of "managing up," that is, managing someone in a position of higher authority. The inverse power relationship can make it difficult for staff to manage board members, especially if the board member is being asked to do something (such as fundraising) that she does not want to do and may resist.

Quite a formidable list — no wonder this is so hard!

Difficult, yes. But not impossible.

SUPPORT YOUR BOARD MEMBERS' INTRINSIC MOTIVATION

A pivotal insight that can help us work more effectively with our board members can be found in new thinking about human motivation. When you hear the word "motivation," what comes to mind? Perhaps a coach giving his team a pep talk before the big game? Or a company setting up incentive bonuses for superior employee performance? That's what is called "extrinsic motivation" — words and actions from one person that are intended to motivate another person to take action.

But as it turns out, *extrinsic* motivation is not as effective as *intrinsic* motivation — motivation that comes from *within* a person. Leading researchers in human motivation[i] have discovered that intrinsic, or self-motivation, is much more effective in influencing behavior.

How can we leverage this to our advantage when engaging board members in fundraising?

First, we can set aside the traditional notion that our task is to "motivate our board members." It's no longer that relevant. Here is the more important question: How can we set up the conditions in which board members will motivate themselves? This is not semantics; it's a game changer. When our framework is to "motivate the board," we might look for ways to "control," e.g., to make board members feel pressured to fundraise, and perhaps guilty if they don't. While pressure and guilt can work to motivate people in the short run, it is less successful in the long run. Here's the better way: adopt a style that affirms the board member's perspective and autonomy. This creates an environment that encourages self-motivation. In practice, this means

- building relationships with board members and listening openly to understand their interests, needs, and concerns. This will help us recognize their individual perspectives and appreciate what they can and want to offer to the organization

- providing opportunities for board members to connect with the mission of our organizations in a personal way

- taking the time to lay out the background and rationale of our fundraising program and the board's role in it

- inviting (rather than pressuring) board members to become involved in fundraising, and offering choices about what their participation can look like

- providing ongoing training, assistance, and support so board members can be successful at the fundraising activities in which they are engaged

The goal is for board members to engage in fundraising activities because *they themselves* see the value in it, have a commitment to it, and can be successful at it — not because we induce them to. Our role as staff is about facilitating that awareness and aspiration. We help board members see the value by engaging them in a conversation about the organization's strategy and future plans and the fundraising activities that support them. We help board members strengthen their commitment by providing opportunities to experience our programs and services in action, and to witness the changes that result. And we help board members be successful by managing the fundraising process and supporting their participation in it.

WHO SHOULD READ THIS BOOK

This book is written for the nonprofit staff members who lead and manage the fundraising programs in their organizations. First and foremost, that's the executive director. Even in organizations with well-staffed development departments, the executive director plays a critical role in providing leadership to the fundraising program and personally being involved in fundraising activities. In lock-step partnership with the executive director, and overseeing the fundraising program, is the development director. The executive director and development director are an important team, and the advice in this book is meant for them to use *together* to engage their board members in the fundraising program in a meaningful way. Board members also might find the book of interest, particularly those who are seeking to spur fundraising activity from their board colleagues. The board environment that I am advocating the staff to create can best be reinforced by the volunteer leadership.

THE ROAD MAP FOR THIS BOOK

Drawing from scores of interviews with nonprofit leaders, this book presents a variety of tested ideas and practices for successfully engaging board members in fundraising. It's not just about doing more, it's also about doing things differently.

Chapter 1 – The Prerequisites

This chapter discusses issues that should be in place before you start to engage your board members in fundraising, such as

- knowing the staff capacity that you plan to invest in supporting your board
- ensuring that you are setting clear expectations about fundraising before individuals join the board
- attaining a baseline level of organizational capacity so that your board has a stable platform from which to engage in fundraising

NOTE: IF YOU HAVE ALREADY ADDRESSED THESE ELEMENTS IN YOUR ORGANIZATION, SKIP THIS CHAPTER AND START AT CHAPTER 2.

Chapter 2 – Connect to Mission

This chapter addresses ways to energize board members by getting them excited about the mission of your organization, such as

- bringing mission moments into board meetings
- framing board discussions around mission
- taking board members to the mission

Chapter 3 – Articulate How Funding Works for Your Organization

This chapter addresses how to establish the context for, and depth of, your organization's fundraising program so that board members can better understand both the big picture and how they can fit in. Topics covered include

- explaining the funding mix
- clarifying roles in the fundraising process
- helping board members own the discussion

Chapter 4 – Build Relationships with Board Members

This chapter focuses on how to build relationships with board members, establish trust, and instill a sense of team. Topics covered include

- working with board members one-on-one
- focusing on key relationships
- cultivating meaningful relationships

Chapter 5 – Create a Structure to Engage Board Members

This chapter presents ideas and suggestions for how to create a structure to enable your board members to successfully engage in fundraising tasks, such as

- creating opportunities for donor and board member interaction
- developing a campaign structure to guide board member participation
- defining what success in fundraising looks like for board members

Chapter 6 – Support Board Members Every Step of the Way

This chapter presents suggestions for how to assist and support your board members to successfully take on their fundraising tasks, such as

- assisting with specific steps of the process
- providing formal and informal training
- recognizing and thanking board members

Appendix – Board Fundraising Toolbox

The appendix contains a set of tools and templates to help jumpstart your work with your board.

Board Fundraising Toolbox
Look for this balloon-shaped box throughout the book for references to the Board Fundraising Toolbox.

WANTED — YOUR FEEDBACK!

I'd love to hear your feedback on this book. If you have suggestions, counterpoints, or personal examples that would make a concept more relevant, or research data related to this topic, I'd love to hear from you. E-mail me at kathyhedge@verizon.net. Thank you in advance!

CHAPTER 1
THE PREREQUISITES

Constructing any solid structure requires a good foundation. Similarly, when building board engagement in fundraising, there need to be certain elements in place before we can successfully start. This section looks at three prerequisites: staff capacity to invest in supporting your board, clarity about fundraising expectations before individuals join the board, and a baseline level of organizational capacity.

KNOW YOUR STAFF CAPACITY TO INVEST

There's no doubt about it — engaging and supporting board members in fundraising requires an ongoing investment of staff time. It's important to plan ahead to ensure that you will be able to provide board members with the staff support they will need as they get more involved in your fundraising efforts. How much staff time to invest depends upon how, and how deeply, you seek to engage your board. And that will depend upon the potential value that the board can add to the fundraising process, given your organization's *fundraising mix* and *board composition*.

Fundraising Mix. Your fundraising mix is the combination of activities that you undertake to raise funds for your organization. Some fundraising activities benefit greatly from board involvement, while others may benefit to a lesser extent. The more your organization relies on fundraising activities that are suited to, and would benefit from, board member involvement, the more it makes sense for you to invest time in engaging your board members in fundraising.

Typically, the fundraising activities that benefit most from board involvement are ones whose success relies on the knowledge of and connection to potential donors, such as major gift programs or corporate outreach. Also, fundraising activities where board members serve as ambassadors for your organization, such as at a special event or conference, benefit from board involvement regardless of a board member's personal connections. Fundraising activities that are staff-driven and that do not depend on personal connections, such as many grantwriting and direct mail programs, do not need as much board member involvement.

Once a donation or grant has been received, board members can be quite productively involved in the thanking process. Studies show that thank you calls from board members influence donors to give again and give more[ii].

The key is to look at the value-added that board members can bring to your particular fundraising activities and to assess how much staff time is warranted, given the potential value.

Questions to consider:

- What fundraising activities does our organization pursue to raise funds? What does it take to make those activities successful? Could our board members help advance those activities in a meaningful way and in ways that staff cannot? How much staff time would be needed to support board members with those activities?
- Are there any threats to our current income streams (fundraising activities or earned income) that would warrant expanding or changing our fundraising mix in the near future? If so, are there new fundraising activities that we would pursue that would rely on or be enhanced by board member involvement?

Board Composition. The amount of time that you invest in your board also relates to your board member makeup — who serves on your board, their contacts and networks, and the skills and attributes they can offer to your fundraising activities. While all board members can play a role in the fundraising process, certain board members will warrant deeper investment of time on your part. For example, board members with connections to business and corporate leaders, foundation leaders, or individuals of wealth can be invaluable in opening doors for your organization. Board members who are willing to tap their own social networks, for example, by holding a house party or social gathering on your organization's behalf, will benefit from your guidance and assistance. While all board members can be involved in some part of the fundraising process, there likely is a subset of your board with which you will invest more significant time.

> *Nonprofit professionals are stressed and never have enough time, so you have to put the majority of your effort into the things that are going to give you the biggest payoff. And that means focusing on board members who have the most connections, the most enthusiasm, and who are the best ambassadors for the organization.*
> — *Lea Harvey, vice president, development, Resources for the Future*

Questions to consider:

- Which board members have contacts or connections with individuals, businesses, or institutions that could be prospective donors? Which board members are willing to tap into their personal networks to assist our fundraising efforts?
- How much staff time would be required to support the board members identified above?
- *With regards to a particular board member:* What are other ways that this board member is contributing (or could contribute) to the organization? How much involvement in fundraising makes sense for this board member given his other contributions to the organization?

BE CLEAR ABOUT FUNDRAISING EXPECTATIONS

Another prerequisite to board involvement in fundraising is setting unambiguous expectations about fundraising before an individual joins the board. It's not just a matter of communicating the general idea of a board's fundraising responsibility — it's about conveying how board members in your organization contribute to the fundraising process.

There are many reasons why we don't address these expectations clearly. Executive directors may feel awkward having the conversation about giving and fundraising because of the power relationship between executive directors and board members; as some will say, "It's like telling your boss what she has to do!" Sometimes, we worry that the "fundraising conversation" will scare off a potential board member. And sometimes we err simply by not being specific enough — we say, "board members are expected to contribute to the fundraising process," but we don't explain what that looks like.

Staff needs to approach the topic of fundraising with board members in a positive, direct, and unapologetic way. Some staff avoid or reluctantly approach the topic of fundraising, which unfortunately reinforces the perception that it is an uncomfortable or intrusive activity to be avoided. Instead, staff can model how to approach the conversation of giving with a donor by fearlessly communicating with their board members about their fundraising responsibilities. — Dan McQuaid, president & CEO, One OC

As uncomfortable as it may be, the board recruitment process is the *best* time to establish a clear understanding of the expectations around "giving and getting." The reaction we don't want to hear later from a board member is, "No one told me I had to do *that!*"

Below are some ways to make sure that we don't gloss over the fundraising conversation and that we recruit board candidates who understand expectations around board giving and fundraising and are ready to get involved.

Create a robust board recruitment process. A good board recruitment process is a two-way street: It helps you determine an individual's passion for your mission and fit with your organization, and it also provides the board candidate with a better sense of your organization and its culture, including its fundraising practices. The Tahirih Justice Center places a strong emphasis on its board recruitment process. Says Executive Director Layli Miller-Muro, "We have a cultivation time frame of one year for people we already know well, and for those we know less well, it's two years — that's how long it will usually take to get to know them to determine if we want to ask them to join the board. This process helps us find people who are really motivated about our organization, for the right reasons. And, during the process, we're very clear about 'giving and getting' expectations, so new board members come in ready to participate in fundraising."

At Volunteers of America of North Louisiana, potential board members are invited to serve on board committees as a first step to board membership. "We try to have board candidates serve on a board committee before joining our board," says Vice President of Communications and Development Lisa Brandeburg. "Since our fundraising model permeates everything we do, including all of our board committees, board candidates who serve on our committees are exposed to our fundraising culture even before they are asked to join the board."

Your board's governance committee (also sometimes called the nominating committee) is a key partner in the recruitment process. Work with your governance committee to be sure that fundraising is one of the dimensions it assesses when evaluating board candidates. This includes considering a person's experience and networks as well as his or her energy and commitment to advancing your cause.

Don't overlook the role your development director can play in identifying potential board members. He or she interacts with donors, community members, and others outside of the organization on a regular basis. Ken Strmiska, vice president for advancement, strategy and innovation at

Lakeland College in Sheboygan, Wisconsin, is highly involved in his college's trustee recruitment process. "We play an important role in trustee recruitment, because we are out there researching and creating relationships with alumni all the time. While capacity to give money isn't the only criterion for who should be on the board of directors, sometimes the financial position that people enjoy is a direct result of how astute and smart they are, which are additional skills and traits that you want in a board member."

Encourage peer conversations. Because of the peer relationship, it is sometimes easier — and more effective — for *board members* to address fundraising expectations with board candidates. This can be done by the board chair, the chair of the board fundraising committee, or a member of the governance committee. Have the board member talk about the ways he is personally involved in fundraising to provide a real-life example. Whichever board members have the conversation, be sure that they are committed to and enthusiastic about board member participation in fundraising. To be sure that the message is delivered clearly, the executive director may want to join the conversation as well.

Provide written examples of specific board fundraising activities. Board job descriptions are helpful in providing a general overview of board responsibilities, but you may want to go one step further when it comes to fundraising. Create a sample list of specific tasks and activities board members undertake to advance fundraising in your organization. This provides a visual that you can hand to a board candidate as you say, "These are examples of what we mean by 'board participation in fundraising.'" It's about making the implicit, explicit. Let candidates know that the range of activities reflect the different strengths and interests of board members. For an example of such a handout that you could share board members, see Tool #1 in the Board Fundraising Toolbox on page 76.

> **Board Fundraising Tool #1**

It's even more powerful if the list is created with board input. For example, the board of Catholic Charities Fort Worth (CCFW) has developed a set of suggested ways that board members can contribute to their fundraising process, such as serving as a table captain at a fundraising event or hosting a dinner in their home for potential donors. Says CCFW CEO Heather Reynolds, "By having something in writing, it's easier for me to have the 'expectations' conversation with prospective board members. And because it was developed *by the board*, at their own instigation, I can say that these are the expectations that board members established for themselves."

100% Board Giving and Setting Minimum Gift Levels

From a fundraising perspective, having a board where all members make a financial contribution to the organization is an important standard to aim for. It's hard to make the case to someone outside the organization to give when those closest to it — board members — have not made their own personal financial donation. And, if board members are involved in asking someone else for a contribution, they need to be able to say that they have already made their own gift. Fortunately, the expectation of 100 percent board giving is becoming more widespread — the 2012 *BoardSource Nonprofit Governance Index* shows that the expectation of full board giving has grown from 47 percent in 1999 to 75 percent in 2012. According to the Nonprofit Research Collaborative's 2012 *Special Report on Engaging Board Members in Fundraising*, 57 percent of responding nonprofit organizations requires a gift by all board members.

Not as widespread is the practice of establishing a minimum gift level for board member contributions. The Nonprofit Research Collaborative's report found that 37 percent of organizations that require a financial contribution from board members have established a minimum gift amount (although percentages varied somewhat based on mission and budget size). Studies conducted for the book *Donor Centered Leadership* found that 12 percent of board members are required to give at or above a certain minimum amount.

Whether or not setting a minimum gift level works for your organization depends on your group's culture and history, but here are some questions for your board and development staff to consider:
· What would be the impact of a minimum gift requirement on the composition of your board? Would you be able to achieve the diversity of composition, perspective, and skill sets that you feel your board needs with this requirement?
· Do you plan to enforce this requirement, and if so, how? If you foresee making some exceptions for the requirement, would this undermine your efforts with other board members?
· Would you be able to achieve the same (or higher) levels of board giving by appealing to each board member individually to contribute on an annual basis?

Here are some alternative ways to communicate to prospective board members that you hope their personal giving will be significant, without setting a minimum amount:
· Ask each board member to make your organization a philanthropic priority.
· Ask each board member that the gift be among his or her top three philanthropic gifts.
· Ask each board member to make a meaningful gift at the top level of his or her philanthropy.

And here's a unique one — DC SCORES in Washington, DC, says, "We would like your gift to be among your top three priority gifts, and that it is significant enough that you have to talk to your partner about it" (in other words, the size of the gift is such that it needs to be in the couple's "financial planning conversation")!

DEMONSTRATE A BASELINE LEVEL OF ORGANIZATIONAL CAPACITY

Another prerequisite for engaging your board in fundraising is to possess a baseline level of organizational capacity so that board members have a firm footing for fundraising. For board members to tap into their networks for potential donors, they need to have confidence in the basic programmatic and operational elements of a nonprofit: a mission and vision that are clear and provide focus, a compelling organizational strategy, quality programs, and a sound financial position.

Without these essentials, enthusiasm can lag. For example, a financial crisis may propel staff to look for ways to get board members more involved in fundraising, but financial woes can actually demotivate fundraising if they are felt to be endemic of structural or strategic issues that need to be addressed first. As Matthew Downey, program director of nonprofit services at Grand Valley State University says, "We have to be willing to recognize other issues within the organization, and that if those issues are not addressed, the fundraising piece will never work. Often, organizations will say, 'Fundraising isn't working for us.' So they will build their fundraising capacity, and go to workshops, and hire consultants and develop a fund development plan. But at the end of the process, if their organizational strategy is still unclear, or if their financial model is weak, they will not be able to improve their fundraising."

Also, the strength of the board overall needs to be considered. Lackluster board meeting attendance or lifeless discussions may require a look at the structure of the board and the quality of board member engagement in general. As Potomac Conservancy President Hedrick Belin says, "If you don't have board engagement writ large, you won't have board engagement in fundraising."

When we evaluated the impact of our multiyear capacity building work, we learned how important it is to help grantees establish essential building blocks before providing fundraising support. When we jumped in prematurely, the results were often lackluster. On the other hand, when we helped organizations lay the ground work that precedes fundraising — ensuring the board deeply understands the mission and that the organization has a clear strategy, direction, funding model, and realistic funding goals — we saw some impressive gains in fundraising, even when that wasn't the main goal of those capacity investments.
— Paula Morris, program director, Flexible Leadership Awards Program, Evelyn & Walter Haas, Jr., Fund

What does board engagement "writ large" look like? It's making board meetings matter by focusing on strategic issues where we need the board's best thinking and input. It's organizing the board's work around key issues and developing a committee structure that is meaningful and productive. It's offering board members a good orientation to your organization and investing in their continuing education to deepen their understanding of your organization's work. It all adds up to harnessing the collective wisdom, talents, and assets of your board members so that they can move your missions forward.

There are many resources that address ways to develop a higher performing board. Some notable ones include the following:

Governance as Leadership by Richard Chait, William Ryan, and Barbara Taylor. This book offers a new framework for boards to do more macro governance and less micromanagement. It sheds new light on the traditional fiduciary and strategic work of the board and introduces a critical third dimension of effective trusteeship: generative governance.

The Practitioner's Guide to Governance as Leadership by Cathy Trower. This book puts the model of *Governance as Leadership* into practice, offering practical guidance on how to nurture a board with high skill and high purpose.

Board Self-Assessment for Nonprofit Boards by BoardSource. Many nonprofit leaders say that self-assessments are the single best way to initiate change with a board, because the process involves board members assessing their own performance. It can lead to a shared understanding of responsibilities and provide a framework for identifying priority areas for improvement.

Ten Basic Responsibilities of Nonprofit Boards: The Companion Workbook by BoardSource. This workbook helps boards understand and enact the core responsibilities of nonprofit boards. It includes questions and group exercises around each responsibility that can be used to spark board discussion and explore topics more deeply.

> *The classic mistake that I've seen nonprofits make over the years is that they just don't do the proper care and feeding of the board. The successful nonprofits have thought about what they want the board to achieve, built the structure, built the committees, and engaged the board with projects that add value. Because if you are going to draw on people's time, they need to see that the time that they have spent has made a difference. A board takes a lot of time and energy, but if properly cared for, it can provide a tremendous return on that investment.*
> — *Joseph Suarez, executive advisor, community partnerships, Booz Allen Hamilton*

CHAPTER 2
CONNECT TO MISSION

When was the last time you asked a board member why she joined the board? Chances are, it wasn't because she enjoys listening to committee reports or attending to Robert's Rules of Order!

Most board members sign on because of their passion for the mission. The key to strengthening board member motivation lies in tapping into that passion and strengthening it. Enthusiasm for the mission enables a board member to overcome fears of fundraising and other obstacles. Board members who raise money do so not because they love fundraising (although some do!), but because they are passionate about our mission and want to advance it.

The power of connecting to the mission may not come as a surprise to you. But what is surprising is how little we focus on it when it comes to our boards and board meetings. And how important it is to building self-motivation.

Where is your board's attention typically focused?

BRING MISSION INTO MEETINGS

Think about the amount of time devoted in board meetings to committee reports, staff reports, and procedural issues — a fiduciary necessity that is seldom uplifting or inspiring. Then think about the excitement of your organization's mission work. Here are some ways that you can make it possible for board members to experience mission during meetings:

Incorporate mission moments into meetings. Take a few minutes of your board meeting to tell a story about how your organization has had an impact. You can invite a client to tell his or her personal story, a staff member can speak about program accomplishments, or better yet, board members can tell their own stories. Many say that the best mission moments are when board members tell their own personal stories about why they got involved in the organization. Says Rev. John W. Swope, S.J., president of Cristo Rey Jesuit High School, "Having mission moments directly helps with fundraising because it reminds everybody why they are there, either by demonstrating to them through a client testimony or having them talk personally about the mission." See the sidebar on page 25 for examples.

Meet at a mission-related location. Choose a location for your board meeting that brings board members closer to your mission. If you can't do this for every meeting, try to do so at least once a year. Consultant Betsy Garside tells of an organization, the Greensgrow Philadelphia Project, where the board traditionally met in an office space in downtown Philadelphia. Says Betsy, "The staff realized that it never saw the board, and suggested that the board start meeting at the farm. Now, every other board meeting is held at the farm so that board members can see the farm in action throughout the year and get a sense of the annual lifecycle of the organization."

> *The most success I ever had with a board was due to their strong connection with the mission and organization. Nothing will move a board faster than a fellow board member who says, 'I really want to see this happen. I'm investing my own money and I'd like you to invest, too.' Too often, we see our board members not giving or getting, and so we decide to create rules and regulations around how it is that they should be engaged. We spend a lot of time doing training and exercises to get them involved, when the reality is, if you can get just a couple of people connected to your vision, they will be behind it and they will get others to support it as well. — Denise Nelson, vice president, resource development, PENCIL*

Frame board discussions around mission. Focus your board meetings — at least some of them — on the issues related to mission, programs, and outreach that brought board members to your organization in the first place. Translating genuine excitement about your program to involvement in fundraising is not a big leap. Consider the following story by Vice President of Development Lea Harvey of Resources for the Future: "In a board meeting, we were briefing our board about our work related to climate policy and a carbon tax. One of our board members became very excited about the topic and really took hold of it. He said, 'I think we really need to maximize this,' so he got together a handful of friends and said, 'I'm putting $100K into this, and I'd like each of you to do the same because this is an organization that can make a difference.' We ended up raising $1 million for the program. How did this happen? By making board meetings focus on mission."

Provide a mission-context to all discussions. It's also possible to transform standard agenda items into opportunities to reinforce mission engagement. Board members benefit from having issues and business decisions presented to them in a mission-context — from reading a financial statement, to evaluating program strategy, to ensuring adequate financial resources for the organization. It connects them to the reason why they joined the organization in the first place. Says consultant Debbie Hechinger, "No matter how much board members participate in meetings, they don't live the organization the way staff do. And if you have a board meeting every three to four months, they are not going to remember what you told them last time. The executive director should always be context-setting and presenting issues within the framework of accomplishing mission and vision." See the sidebar on page 26 for a story of how one nonprofit, Cristo Rey Jesuit High School of Baltimore, infuses mission into everything it does.

One of the benefits of strategic planning for board members is that it engages them around a common vision to the point that they recognize that they each have a role in reaching that vision — that we are all in this together. And it gives them the motivation to stretch themselves to figure out what their particular role will be.
— Sharon Spira-Cushnir, COO, St. Anne's

Involve boards in the development and monitoring of strategic plans. A strategic planning process is framed around articulation and accomplishment of mission. Boards should be heavily involved in the organization's strategic planning process, and in the ongoing monitoring of the successful implementation

Mission Moments

"Once we had the chief scientist of the Grand Teton National Park do a short presentation to our board about wildlife issues in the Park, a program that our foundation totally funds. We weren't looking at any budgets or forecasts; we were just feeling good about what we do. Here was our chief scientist saying, 'We couldn't do this without you,' and really meaning it. The board felt so good! It gave them a connection to the power of what we're doing." — Leslie Mattson, Grand Teton National Park Foundation

"Two things that we do at every board and committee meeting: 1) we tell a story about how we have had an impact, and 2) we share our fundraising gap for that year. We'll say 'our gap for this year is X, and right now we're Y% of the way there'. So we make everyone aware of our impact, and of our current gap. Those two things tend to get everybody engaged." — Lisa Brandeburg, Volunteers of America of North Louisiana

"What we found that works well for a 'mission moment' is to ask board members to share why they joined the organization. You can do this when a new board member joins the board, both as a 'get-to-know-you' exercise and to reaffirm everyone's personal commitment. Let the board members tell stories about the work, and encourage them to share their perspective on the story and what really moved them." — Paula Morris, program director, Flexible Leadership Awards Program, Evelyn & Walter Haas, Jr., Fund of that plan. Board meetings can include regular opportunities to revisit the plan and assess progress.

Involving board members in strategic planning has another side benefit for fundraising — it's a great way to help board members be more articulate about the needs, strategies, and programmatic work of your organization, which are the same topics they will address with potential donors. The more knowledgeable board members are about your organization and the needs you address, the more motivated and successful they will be in fundraising.

SPOTLIGHT ON BOARD PRACTICE
The Board Mission Identity Committee

One nonprofit that is very disciplined about staying focused on mission is Cristo Rey Jesuit High School in Baltimore, Maryland. It has formed a standing board committee called the Mission Identity Committee, which monitors how the mission is integrated into the school and to make sure the school avoids 'mission creep.' The committee is also charged with ongoing formation of board members around the mission of the school and of identifying mission moments for board meetings.

Recently, the Mission Identity Committee started meeting with other committees of the board, which has reinforced how the work of each committee supports the mission. As another way to reinforce mission, the board decided that every board resolution, on whatever topic, has to be accompanied by a statement on how the resolution will advance the mission of the school. Says Rev. John W. Swope, S.J., president of Cristo Rey Jesuit, "I like that the mission is really demanding on all aspects of the school. It's a responsibility we have to all of our benefactors and to the community that we make all of our decisions based primarily on mission." This focus on mission also provides an ongoing motivation for the board, because they are continually provided with the context about why their fundraising efforts are so important and what those efforts accomplish.

TAKE BOARD MEMBERS TO THE MISSION

Your organization's programmatic work is being delivered somewhere other than the boardroom. Give your board members an opportunity to experience your organization's mission hands-on. Here are some ideas:

Visit project sites. Some organizations plan project site visits for board members so that they can experience the mission in action. Steve Richards, board member of Sustainable Harvest International (SHI), says his board has one meeting each year in one of the Central American countries where the organization works. Says Steve, "While we are there, we meet the farmers whom we are supporting, we meet their families, and we see how they are using the tools and training that SHI has provided. It's highly motivating. We know if we raise more money, we can serve more farmers and save more forests from being burned."

Showing the impact that an organization is having, and what more could be done with additional funds, is highly motivating for a board. — Steve Richards, board member, Sustainable Harvest International

---

Provide volunteer opportunities. Some nonprofits encourage board members to volunteer and design volunteer opportunities specifically for board members. Says CEO Heather Reynolds of Catholic Charities Fort Worth, "We ask our board members to attend a board service activity each year where they can actively engage with our clients. This invigorates their passion and helps them understand what we do on the ground every day." American Red Cross board member Charlotte Berry says, "Several of our board members — especially new ones who don't have a long history with the organization — have gone out on local disaster calls, and they come back to the board meeting and report on what they've seen. They are really moved by the experience. Board members aren't required to go on these calls, but more and more want to now that they've seen the initial group come back with such enthusiasm."

Plan a retreat or board social activity with a mission focus. Holding a board retreat or social gathering has many benefits, including taking the board members to a place where they can experience the mission up close. Says President Hedrick Belin of the Potomac Conservancy, "We have many opportunities for board members to get together, see what our organization does, and appreciate the need we serve. One of these opportunities is a standing monthly hike for both existing and former board members. I often learn more from board members on these hikes than anywhere else!"

Give board members their stories. When you provide board members with opportunities to connect to the mission, you also give them a chance to develop their own stories about the organization. Red Cross board member Charlotte Berry's account of her fellow board members' volunteer experience on a disaster call is a case in point. Those board members now can tell others about their own personal experience in helping victims of a

How the St. Mary's Hospital Board Got Their Stories

— *Matthew Downey, Nonprofit Services Program Director, Johnson Center for Philanthropy at Grand Valley State University*

"When I was a young staff member at St. Mary's Hospital for Children in Queens, we had a very powerful NYC-based board. As staff, we were frustrated that our board wasn't as engaged in fundraising as we hoped they would be. We had regular board meetings and frequent individual meetings with board members, but we weren't seeing a lot of enthusiasm and motivation among them.

"One day, it occurred to us that perhaps the board didn't have enough contact with the people we were serving. So we decided to create an opportunity for board members to get their stories. Here's what we did: At the next board meeting, we threw out the regular agenda, and we set up stations all over the hospital — stations in occupational therapy, physical therapy, speech therapy, art therapy, music therapy, recreational therapy...you name the therapy, we had a station. We split the board members into teams of three, sent them off on different paths, and told them that they had to go through the hospital and interact with the therapists and children at each station. At the art therapy station, they did a little art therapy project with the kids and therapist. At the speech therapy station, they had to see how speech therapists teach preemie infants how to suck, and then they had to wash their hands and do the same massaging technique on the lips that therapists did. This went on for about two hours, and then we brought them back to the boardroom. Now, these were professional men and women — tough New Yorkers. And they sat in that boardroom, and they cried. They were just overwhelmed by what they had seen. And as they left the boardroom that evening the staff looked at each other and said, 'OK, now they have their stories.'

"Shortly thereafter, we began noticing an uptick in the number of calls we received from board members saying that they had a friend who might be interested in getting involved with St. Mary's. The conversation would go something like this: A board member would say, 'I have a friend who's my neighbor, and I saw him while I was mowing the lawn the other day, and I got to talking to him about the children's hospital, and he wants to come in for a tour.' You see, the board members had connected to the mission in such a powerful way that they couldn't stop thinking about it. And if you can't stop thinking about it, you can't stop talking about it. So when you are out mowing your lawn and your neighbor comes over, and you still have this visual image of the kid in the pediatric traumatic brain injury unit whom you helped in music therapy by shaking a rattle with him, that visual image doesn't go away. You keep talking about it, even to your neighbor when you're mowing the lawn. That's what board members need — they need to be blown away by the power of our mission, to see that fundraising is not talking about money, it's talking about those kids."

disaster. This is key to fundraising. One of the most effective ways to get others excited about the work of your organization is to tell a compelling story. And it's easier, and more genuine, if the story is your own. As ambassadors and spokespersons, board members need their own stories. See the box on the preceeding page to learn how board members got their stories at St. Mary's Hospital for Children in Queens, New York.

CHAPTER 3

ARTICULATE HOW FUNDING WORKS FOR YOUR ORGANIZATION

Remember the fable of the elephant and the blind men? A group of blind men come upon an elephant and seek to learn what it is like. They each touch a part of the elephant, but only one part. The man who feels the trunk thinks the elephant is like a serpent. The man who feels the tusk thinks the elephant is like a spear. And so on. Though each man was partly right, on the whole, they were all wrong.

If you focus on a single part, you miss the big picture.

For board members to effectively participate in fundraising, they need to understand the big picture of how our organization is funded. Understanding the organization's funding mix, that is, the combination of earned and contributed revenue that finances our programs and services, enables board members not only to make good programmatic and financial decisions, but it gives them a context for their own participation in fundraising.

When board members understand how funding and fundraising work — the strategies, investment needed, who does what, and what it takes to succeed — they can understand their own role more clearly. Involving board members in a discussion of the funding model and the unique role that they play in it is a powerful tool for board engagement.

EXPLAIN THE FUNDING MIX

Listed below are the elements to cover as you present your funding mix to your board. Figure 1 on page 34 provides an illustration of what the process looks like and questions to address with your board members.

Create a bridge from mission to money. As highlighted in Chapter 2, mission motivates self-action. While your conversation with your board about the funding mix will focus on funding, acknowledge that funding is not an end in itself — it provides the fuel needed to run the programs and services that advance your mission. By grounding the conversation around mission, you create a bridge between passion for programs and action around fundraising.

Demonstrate the translation of mission to money by explaining which revenue streams fund which programs and services. For example, a government contract may cover the direct costs of an after-school youth program, and a special event may raise unrestricted funds that cover the program's indirect costs. In this case, both revenue streams fund different aspects of the same program; laying this out clarifies the relevance and roles of both.

Articulate the revenue streams. Many nonprofit organizations rely on a combination of earned income (e.g., fee for service, ticket sales for performances, government contracts) and contributions (e.g., annual giving program, major gifts program, special events) to fund their organizations. It is helpful for board members to understand how both earned income and contributions fund the organization. A board member may mistakenly think that if an organization collects fees for services, its fundraising needs are not that great. Explain the percentage of total revenue that each source provides, and the type of funding that each represents (e.g., restricted or unrestricted funds; annual, capital, or endowment funds).

> *The most effective place to start the fundraising conversation with the board is to help them understand how funding works for their organization — the mix of funding sources, the business model, the goals, the structure. You do this before you address what they can do. My experience is that organizations often start by working with the board on what they can do to help raise money, before discussing the organization's funding model and their role as stewards and partners in making the fundraising successful. — Paula Morris, program director, Flexible Leadership Awards Program, Evelyn & Walter Haas, Jr., Fund*

Next, drill down to take a closer look at contributions raised through the combination of fundraising activities that your organization undertakes (that is, your fundraising program). Many board members may be familiar with one aspect of your fundraising program, such as a special event or direct mail, but they may not know or understand the full scope of all of your fundraising activities and how they work together. Mapping out your fundraising program provides an opportunity for you to get really clear about how you raise funds, and to demonstrate to the board that fundraising is a multi-step process of building relationships with individuals and institutions, not a one-time "ask" for money.

Clarify roles. As part of mapping out your fundraising program, you should also be clear about what it takes to succeed, and on the roles the executive director, the development staff, and the board members play to achieve that success. Be sure to highlight where board members can add the most value to the fundraising program, and explain how the staff support board members in the process. The idea is to help your board members understand how your fundraising program works and what it takes to make it successful (which is really important if one of the key success factors is board member participation!).

Says Cleveland Museum of Art Deputy Director and Chief Advancement Officer August Napoli, "You want to show board members where they fit into the larger fundraising program. So, they have to understand what the larger program is. You show that everyone has a role in the program, and that, 'We can't do this part without you, Mr. or Ms. Trustee.'"

Help boards understand the investment of resources needed. It's also important to help board members understand the investment of human and other resources that are needed to make the fundraising program

Assessing Your Funding Model

As part of the dialogue with your board about your funding mix, you may want to assess the effectiveness of your overall funding model, including your fundraising activities. Below are some resources to help you with that task.

- "Finding Your Funding Model" by Peter Kim, Gail Perreault, and William Foster, *Stanford Social Innovation Review,* Fall 2011.
- *Nonprofit Sustainability* by Jeanne Bell, Jan Masaoka, and Steve Zimmerman, Jossey Bass, 2010.
- "Ten Nonprofit Funding Models" by William Foster, Peter Kim, and Barbara Christiansen, *Stanford Social Innovation Review,* Spring 2009.

Where I have found the greatest success is helping the board understand the depth and breadth of fundraising. I start by showing how the fundraising program supports the priority needs of the institution and our overall vision. Then I talk about the specifics of the fundraising program, so that they understand that fundraising is much more than just 'asking' for money. I talk about the staff driven activities, and I help them see where they as board members will be of greatest value. This way, they don't feel like they have the responsibility for the whole program. It's like an orchestra. Every instrument has its value and purpose. Independently, they are nice; collectively, they are magnificent.
— August Napoli, Jr., deputy director and chief advancement officer, Cleveland Museum of Art

---

successful. Many development staff say that they are often asked to raise funds to meet budget goals that they have little input in, and often without the resources needed to meet those goals[iii]. A comprehensive dialogue with your board about fundraising presents an opportunity to discuss achievable financial goals and the resources needed to meet those goals.

Figure 1: Presenting the Funding Mix to Your Board

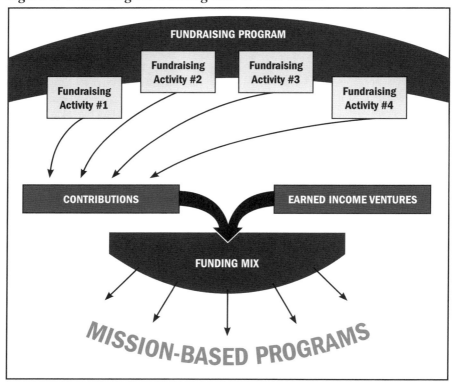

Possible Questions for Analysis:

- How much money is raised by each fundraising activity? What percent of contributions does each activity represent? What is the cost per dollar raised for each activity?
- How much of the funds raised are unrestricted versus restricted? Which programs do the restricted funds apply to?
- How do the different fundraising activities relate to or depend upon each other? Do any of the activities offer mission-related benefits? Other benefits?

- What are the interdependencies between each fundraising activity and other parts of the organization?
- How does each fundraising activity work? What are its critical success factors?
- Who are the donors that each fundraising activity reaches? Why do they give?
- What are the staffing and other resources needed for each fundraising activity?
- Where can board members add the greatest value to this fundraising activity? How will they be supported by staff?
- What are the strengths, weaknesses, opportunities, and threats for each fundraising activity?

HELP YOUR BOARD OWN THE DISCUSSION

While all boards benefit from having a better understanding of the organization's funding mix, it is especially helpful to provide this context if you are introducing change, such as a change in your fundraising program or a change in the expectation of how and to what extent your board members are involved in fundraising. In cases of change, the *way* in which you approach and address your board about the fundraising program is as important as the information conveyed. Use a method that solicits input, provides analysis, and builds board member understanding. When people understand how something works and why it is important, and when they have had an opportunity to give input and feedback, they will be more invested in the final results.

Consider the following story from Vice President for Resource Development Denise Nelson at the nonprofit PENCIL: "Last year, for the first time, we had a shortfall in funds raised at our gala, which is the main source of our contributed income. So the board decided to form a resource development committee to look at how the board should be more involved in fundraising. I think the rest of the board thought that the committee and staff would come back with a list of names for each board member to contact, but instead we decided to start by taking a step back. Over the next three board meetings, we presented an analysis of the organization's fundraising history, our current fundraising channels, and how other organizations approach board giving and fundraising. We didn't present new fundraising ideas as 'This is what we want to institute here.' Instead, we said, 'As part of our due diligence, we want to share with you some of our findings.' So we showed them the fundraising practices and policies of other peer nonprofit organizations, and we explained the reasons why they follow those practices. Board members asked questions and gave input, and members of the resource development committee also shared their thoughts about the findings and what they thought might work for our organization. At a subsequent board meeting, the resource development committee proposed a new board fundraising model, which was approved. So we followed a slow but steady process of building understanding and allowed plenty of time for people to ask questions and give feedback. In the end, the change went forward because it was really a 'no-brainer' at that point — people felt like it made sense and was the logical solution."

By following a process that allowed the full board to become more knowledgeable about fundraising and provided opportunities for input, the PENCIL staff and resource development committee helped ensure that the board was comfortable with the model that was eventually proposed. Getting board buy-in for something that is new (and for something that is perceived as difficult, as fundraising often is) is not easy, and sometimes you may need to focus on recruiting new board members to move the fundraising conversation forward. But in many instances, good process can make the difference.

Here's how you can develop an approach that can lead to board member buy-in for your fundraising program and their participation in it:

Find your board champions for fundraising. Start the dialogue about fundraising with your board leadership and those who are most supportive of fundraising, such as the board fundraising committee chair or committee members. These board members can provide valuable input on the fundraising program and how it is presented to the full board. The support of this initial group of board members is critical, so view them as partners. Your full board discussion about your fundraising program and the board's role in it will be much better received if the conversation is being led by other board members rather than the staff.

Prep board members early and often. It's helpful for board members to have an opportunity to digest an idea before discussing it at a board meeting. Some board members may feel more comfortable fleshing out an idea in a smaller group or one-on-one with the executive director, development director, or committee chair first. This gives them familiarity with the issue so that they can participate more productively in the boardroom discussion. Says President Hedrick Belin of the Potomac Conservancy, "To make sure that my board members really understand

and own the fundraising discussion, I give them multiple ways to learn and discuss the issues before the board meetings. My development director and I have drafted concept papers with ideas around fundraising that we've shared individually with board members to get their feedback. We've done this with the board fundraising committee as well. So when we take the issue to the full board meeting, it has already been vetted by several board members. This helps them to be able to take a lead in the discussion."

> Very often, it can't be the director of development or even executive director leading the conversation with the board about its involvement in fundraising. This is why the development committee is so important, because it's usually the head of that committee who takes charge. And he or she will say to the board, "I'm leading this effort and you have to hang in there with me." So it's a peer-to-peer conversation.
> — Jane O'Connell, president, Altman Foundation

Widen the scope of your "Development Report." Board meetings often include a presentation of a development or fundraising report. Use this time to educate board members about the bigger fundraising picture, e.g., trends, opportunities, risks. Says Resources for the Future Vice President of Development Lea Harvey, "In my development reports to the board, I present much more than just the numbers against goals. It's more of an analysis of how we are doing based on the current landscape and where we see it going. I also highlight the risks and opportunities we see emerging. And this is presented within the context of the strategic goals of the organization. So it's not just numbers in isolation, it's about providing a basic understanding of fundraising and how it ties to programmatic goals."

Tap into outside expertise. Consider bringing in a consultant or board member from a similar nonprofit to talk to your board about different fundraising activities and what board member engagement looks like in each. Some nonprofits have reported that an outside consultant with fundraising expertise and no personal stake in the outcome brings more credibility to the discussion.

CHAPTER 4

BUILD RELATIONSHIPS WITH BOARD MEMBERS

Building a good rapport with board members is another important way to engage them in fundraising (and in the organization in general). Strong relationships build camaraderie, establish trust, and instill a feeling of "team." It's all about supporting the need to belong, which is a key driver in psychological theories of leading thinkers such as Abraham Maslow and Alfred Adler.[iv] When people feel a part of a group, they are more open to the norms and practices of the group — including the practice of fundraising.

WORK WITH BOARD MEMBERS ONE-ON-ONE

Boards don't fundraise, *board members do.* By reaching out to board members separately, we help them determine how our organization's fundraising program best relates to them based on their own personal strengths and interests. As St. Anne's COO Sharon Spira-Cushnir says, "There are things that you need to do at the whole board level, but then you need to customize it down to the individual board member. You might come up with 'the plan' as a board, but then the staff needs to have an individual conversation with board members to determine what each is going to do from that plan on a one-on-one level. In the full group, everyone will say, 'Yes, this is great, this is what we should all do,' but then you need to translate that to the individual person."

Spending time with board members individually provides an opportunity to get to know each of them better and learn their interests and perspectives. Active listening is the best approach. The better we understand our board members, the better we can help them find ways to participate in fundraising that works for them and can be successful.

Below are examples of different techniques for approaching a one-on-one conversation with board members.

Have a get-to-know-you conversation. The staff at United Neighborhood Houses (UNH) takes proactive steps to get to know board members before engaging them in fundraising. Says Executive Director Nancy Wackstein, "When (UNH Director of Development) Jessica Ziegler came here, no one was tasked with getting to know the board members. I did know them, but I had limited time, so I didn't have time to find out things such as who they knew, what networks they belong to, and what they like to do. We created Jessica's position so that we would have the capacity on staff to really get to know our board members and work with them individually. Jessica meets with each board member to get a read on who they are, their interests, and what they understand about what the organization does. Jessica has been able to match board members and their skills to mission-related volunteer opportunities as well as fundraising opportunities, which board members like. It's not just about fundraising. People want to feel that they aren't just there to raise money." Says Jessica, "It starts with an interview at the beginning. I have a list of questions that I ask about their family, their interests, their education, and their involvement with other nonprofits. So it gives me ideas about who they might know and ways that they can participate in fundraising that they themselves may not have realized. In talking with them, I might come up with ten ideas that don't work, but then I'll come up with one that really works, so it pays off to have this conversation with board members." For a sample of get-to-know-you questions that you can ask current or prospective board members, see Tool #2 in the Board Fundraising Toolbox on page 78.

> I think everybody has to be involved in fundraising, if you define it as a process and not an event. I worked with the Chief Justice of the Missouri Supreme Court, and she told me that by law, she couldn't be involved in fundraising. I asked her if she could thank donors, and she said, "Absolutely." To me, that's being involved in fundraising. She had stationery with the Supreme Court seal on it, and she wrote thank-you notes on that stationery. People kept them for years. They really valued her thank you.
> — Carol Weisman, consultant

Board Fundraising Tool #2

Offer a menu for involvement. Individuals come to board service with their own skills, interests, and strengths. They will be most motivated when you take the time at the outset to design an engagement plan that suits them. Avoid "one size fits all" solutions. Consultant Carol Weisman calls this the "Chess versus Checkers School of Fundraising™." Carol explains, "When you play a game of checkers, every piece is the same size and moves in the same direction. And this is where many nonprofits fail with their boards. They start a sentence by saying, 'Everybody needs to do

X, where the X might be selling 10 tickets to the organization's upcoming gala. But it never happens, because not everyone has the same capacity. I much prefer the game of chess as an analogy because different pieces are different sizes and they move in different directions. That doesn't mean you don't have to play by the rules of the game, but you use people effectively. So if I have someone who can sell 150 tickets to the gala, and someone else who can give a speech at his or her church, why would I ask everyone to sell 10 tickets? The ground rule is everybody has to be involved." For a list of examples that illustrate a range of ways board members can be involved in fundraising, see Tool #3 in the Board Fundraising Toolbox on page 79.

Board Fundraising Tool #3

Integrate program and fundraising needs. When possible, connect board members to fundraising activities for programs that they have a particular passion for. Engage board members in a holistic conversation about the program, including its funding needs. Says Resources for the Future Vice President of Development Lea Harvey, "Our senior team and executive director go through our list of board members and identify opportunities for engaging each of them, based on our knowledge of their interest and background related to our research projects. We look for ways that board members can assist us with research projects but also with the fundraising, events, and communications related to those projects. Then we have different staff reach out to different board members. For example, I often team up with one of our researchers or program staff to meet with a board member about a particular project. We'll ask for the board member's advice on our work, whom we can solicit for support, and if and how he or she can help in that process. So it's not purely a fundraising conversation, it's also a programmatic conversation."

FOCUS ON KEY RELATIONSHIPS

While all relationships are important, some are more critical than others. This section takes a look at some of the key relationships that we need to focus on to set the stage for successful board member engagement in fundraising.

Executive Director and Director of Development
Since the executive director has the primary relationship with board members in general, and the director of development oversees the fundraising program, the relationship between the two is perhaps the most critical in determining the success of board member engagement in

fundraising. Although their fundraising roles vary and overlap at times, the executive director typically provides the leadership to fundraising and the director of development supervises the management of it. The executive director sets the tone, generates enthusiasm, and models support for the fundraising process, in part by being the public face of the institution with major donors and others. With respect to the board, the executive director demonstrates his or her support of the development director by being a vocal advocate for fundraising and by providing the development director with access to board members.

The development director oversees the planning and implementation of the fundraising process and provides guidance to the executive director, board members and others who interact with donors. The big issues of determining the fundraising mix and strategy are usually determined by the executive director and development director together.

Executive directors tend to go in one of two directions. Some like to have exclusive relations with their boards. There are others, including me, who strongly believe in connecting key staff to the board of directors, because the key staff can be better at articulating the needs and issues that they oversee. Our development director has strong, independent relationships with board leaders, so she can articulate development needs directly and effectively. My basic belief is that you have to trust your staff leaders — the executive director does, and the board does. This isn't my show; this is our show. We all roll together to make this work happen. — Craig Shniderman, executive director, Food & Friends

Despite the pivotal nature of this relationship, many organizations struggle with it. In the 2013 report, *UnderDeveloped: A National Study of Challenges Facing Nonprofit Fundraising*, only 41 percent of development directors say they have a strong relationship with the executive director, and 21 percent the relationship is "weak" or "poor."[v]

It falls on both the executive director and development director to form a partnership based on trust and respect so that they can work as a unified team with the board. For the executive director, this includes building opportunities for the development director to interact with board members (see box on page 45 for specific ways to do this). Says Paula Morris, program director of the Flexible Leadership Awards Program at the Evelyn & Walter Haas, Jr., Fund, "We have seen organizations where the executive director wants to own the relationship with the board so much that the development director has no exposure or connection to the board, and then the development director is only called upon when it's time for that cajoling, 'You haven't done this yet,' role with the board."

For the development director, this includes demonstrating competency and reliability as well as an understanding of the executive director's priorities and interests. Says Resources for the Future Vice President of Development Lea Harvey, "You can't be threatening in any way to the executive director, and you have to be very aware of what you are doing and how your actions might be perceived. To gain the confidence of the executive director, you have to demonstrate that you really understand all of the dynamics of your fundraising program and the environment in which you are operating."

The development director also engenders confidence by providing the executive director with a similar level of high-quality support in fundraising that she provides to board members. Says Taxpayers for Common Sense Director of Development Jen Cox, "I try to remember that my executive director is not thinking about fundraising all day. She's got 100 other things to do, and it's my job to see that the fundraising tasks are done, so if that means scheduling 10 minutes on her calendar to make these three fundraising-related decisions with her, then that is what I need to do. And similar to the way I work with board members, I will draft the e-mail that she needs to send to a donor and not simply wait for her to do it. It's just good staffing. Over time, she gains more trust in me — she trusts my work, my tone, and my point of view — which gives her confidence to provide more opportunities for me to interact with board members."

> *The CEO and development director have a yin-yang relationship — complementary and interdependent. To truly be successful when it comes to the board, the CEO will want to give the development director access to board members. And the development director must manage those relationships with integrity, keeping the CEO apprised. It's a two-way street of trust and respect.*
> — *Kathleen Rae King, former national vice president for development, Volunteers of America*

Board Chair and Board Fundraising Committee Chair

The board chair and/or the chair of the board fundraising committee provide the peer leadership for fundraising, modeling enthusiasm and promoting participation among other board members. (The leadership may also come from a vice-chair or other fundraising committee members as well.) Paula Morris, program director of the Flexible Leadership Awards Program at the Evelyn & Walter Haas, Jr., Fund, has observed that the most effective board engagement happens "when you have a team of three really working well together — first, the development director and executive director working well together, and then the board chair or another board champion. When there is a real champion on the board for that work, that's when you have board engagement. If it's the executive director pushing it without a board champion, that is difficult."

Your board fundraising leader(s) need to have a strong relationship with both the executive director and development director, but also with other board members. They will be more influential with their peers if they are known and respected by them. St. Anne's COO Sharon Spira-Cushnir illustrates this point with the following story of an organization she worked at earlier in her career: "It was the early part of the recession, and our two board vice-chairs helped me create a plan to engage the board more in fundraising. We came up with a great plan and agreed that the two of them would call all the board members to discuss the ways we had come up with for engaging the board in fundraising. Everything was fine until I sent them their list of board members to contact. They both said to me, 'Sharon, I don't really know these people, it's a weird thing for me to call them. If you really want me to, I will, but you would get further with this than I will, because the board members don't really know me like they know you.' I realized that they felt that they did not have the social capital with the other board members to have this conversation. This was a wake-up call that we needed to create more opportunities for board members to get to know each other."

Board Fundraising Committee

A board fundraising committee (or fund development committee) is typically composed of board members ready, or at least willing, to advance the organization's fundraising efforts and to encourage other board members to do so. The existence of the committee provides a way for board members who are most adept at fundraising to self-identify. They help shape the fundraising strategy and model, encourage full board engagement in fundraising, and provide guidance to staff on the best ways to engage other board members. While a board should not delegate all fundraising activity solely to members of the fundraising committee, these members are often the most involved in fundraising. Building relationships with fundraising committee members (and forming such a committee if it doesn't exist already) should be a top priority for the development director.

For an in-depth look at the function and structure of the board fundraising committee, see BoardSource's book *Development Committee* by Eugene Tempel, at www.boardsource.org.

Building Opportunities for Development Director Interaction with Board Members

It's helpful to identify and create opportunities for your development director to interact with board members. Below is a list of ideas on how to get started.

- **Ensure the Development Director Attends Board Meetings.** It is critical that development directors attend board meetings — not just development committee meetings, but full board meetings. Board meetings provide development directors with important insights about key organizational issues and the perspectives of board members. It gives board members an opportunity to gain confidence in the development director and to be more comfortable working with him/her outside of meetings. The mere presence of the development director in the meeting highlights the importance and centrality of development within the organization.

- **Include the Development Director in Meetings with Board Members and Board Candidates.** Look for ways to include the development director in meetings and functions that involve board members, individually and as a group. Some executive directors involve development directors in board candidate interviews, which allows development directors to begin to develop a relationship with that candidate early on. Others include their development directors along in meetings with specific board members to discuss fundraising and other issues. Still others give development directors specific board-related responsibilities, such as updating board members on key issues. This kind of inclusion by the executive director sends a signal to the board that the executive director values and trusts the development director, so it can too.

- **Set Up a Mentor-Mentee Relationship Between Your Board Champion for Fundraising and Your Development Director.** For executive directors with development directors who are relatively early in their career, it can be helpful to ask a board member who is knowledgeable about, and supportive of, fundraising to serve as a mentor for your development director. The development director will gain important knowledge and also have a natural way to develop a relationship with a key proponent of fundraising on the board (and it can be rewarding for the board member too).

CULTIVATE MEANINGFUL RELATIONSHIPS

Below are some key reminders about building strong relationships with board members.

Make it intentional. Relationship building with board members doesn't just happen — especially if they live in different geographic areas — it requires planning. It also helps when we approach relationship-building from a perspective of openness and genuine interest in getting to know board members and learning about their ideas. Potomac Conservancy President Hedrick Belin describes how he approaches this issue: "I meet with my board chair once a month, and we look at a spreadsheet that lists all of our board members vertically, with the months of the year in the horizontal columns. We plan how we will connect with each board member for the coming few months. Perhaps it's a committee meeting, or maybe we will pay a visit to that person. We look at what and when the board member is hearing from us in between our quarterly board meetings. And it's not just an engagement strategy — these are really smart people, so I *want* to tap their knowledge and expertise."

Invest in face time. Many executive directors communicate with their board members primarily via e-mail and at board meetings. There are times when those methods are fine, but there is no substitute for face-to-face and phone meetings for building a real relationship. Says Matthew Downey, program director, nonprofit services, Grand Valley State University, "One of my mentors was an executive director who had a list of board members by her phone, and every time she spoke with a board member she would mark the date down. If too much time elapsed and she had not had contact with a board member either by phone or in person, she would get on the phone and schedule time with that board member. You have to do that, because you have to have dialogue to build relationship. The skilled executive director will ask questions to build an understanding of that board member's interests, skills, and network, and from there you connect the dots for fund development."

Match the formality with the occasion. Sometimes executive directors err on the side of being too formal and business-like with board members, assuming that "more formal" equals "more professional." There are certainly times when formality is needed, but there are other times where you can be less formal. Sometimes a less formal connection can feel more "real." Says consultant Debbie Hechinger, "The more personal the contact, the more human the relationship, the better it is. To some extent, the more informal you are, the more you create a feeling of partnership. It's OK for executive directors to sometimes speak in more personal, emotive ways and tap into people's hearts. After all, that's why board members are there — because they believe in the mission and vision, and that comes from the heart."

Be open and transparent. It's important to share both good news and bad news with board members. This is critical for building trust. Food & Friends Executive Director Craig Shniderman says, "One of the first things I say to a new board president is, 'My pledge to you is that you'll never hear good news or bad news first from someone else.' I don't like sharing bad news, but you want candor and you want trust with your board, so you have to be consistent and forthright so that no one has a sense of wondering." Fostering a culture of openness and transparency is critical for both staff and board members to feel confident in the organization as they embark on fundraising activities. Says Rev. John W. Swope, S.J., president of Cristo Rey Jesuit High School, "Our board appreciates directness, honesty, and transparency when something isn't going right. They expect to hear both the good and the bad, and we tell them the good and the bad. This gives them a comfort level for fundraising."

> *Providing opportunities for board members to socialize is really important. One of the things I've learned in chairing board fundraising efforts for many years is that it is very helpful to provide opportunities for board members to work together and experience their fundraising efforts together as a group. And the social piece is mixed with that. If board members have a chance to get to know each other, they will work together more effectively.*
> *— Charlotte Berry, board member, United Way Association of South Carolina*

Make time for social exchange. Board meetings tend to be so packed with board business that there is little room for socializing. Foster a sense of community among board members by planning occasional board retreats, mission outings, and social opportunities. These provide an important time for board members to connect socially with each other, with the staff, and with the mission. For examples of social and volunteer opportunities for board members, see Tool #4 in the Board Fundraising Toolbox on page 82.

> **Board Fundraising Tool #4**

CHAPTER 5

CREATE A STRUCTURE TO ENGAGE BOARD MEMBERS

Up to now, this book has focused primarily on how to set up the conditions in which board members will become motivated to engage in fundraising. This chapter shifts to identifying ways to enable board members to fundraise. It's about creating structured opportunities for board members to be involved in your fundraising program, making it easy for them to "plug in."

Says Heather Reynolds, CEO of Catholic Charities Fort Worth, "Too often, nonprofit staff talk to their boards about what they want the end result to be, such as 'We need your help in raising $50,000 for this new program.' But then they don't break it down into small steps. If you want someone to contribute to your organization, the first step might be to get that person to come out and take a tour of your facility. It's much clearer to board members if you ask them to invite their friends to come to a tour, rather than saying, 'Please introduce your friends to our organization.' So it's important to create a specific volunteer opportunity, and it's also important to have an overall structure to your program so that they know how inviting a friend to a tour fits into the big picture."

> We don't often break down in extremely specific ways what it means when we say to the board, "We need your participation in fundraising." We just say "go fundraise" but we don't tell them what we mean by that.
>
> — Mathew Downey, program director, nonprofit services, Grand Valley State University

HELP BOARD MEMBERS PLUG IN

Listed below are ways to guide board member involvement in fundraising. Not all ideas will work for all organizations, so factor in your organization's mission, culture, community, and board composition. Keep in mind, too, the opportunity cost associated with whatever you ask board members to do. Board members have limited time, so be sure that you ask each board member to help in the way where he can add the most value.

Create opportunities for board members to cultivate donors. One way to enable board members to advance your fundraising is to create events for donors that introduce them to your organization and let them experience your mission. These could be tours, open houses, lectures, presentations — any type of event or program that showcases the work of your organization. At these events, your board members serve as ambassadors. Staff has the responsibility for planning and organizing these events, and the board member's role focuses on identifying, inviting, and talking with guests. Having the event "on the calendar" creates a timeline and a sense of urgency that can help propel board members (and staff) to action. To see how one nonprofit, Volunteers of America of North Louisiana, has developed a fundraising program that relies heavily on board member participation in donor cultivation events, see Case Study #1 on page 52.

Especially effective are activities where donors can experience your mission up close. Look for opportunities to create an activity for donors (such as a reception, dinner, or other gathering) around one of your organization's programs or services (such as a seminar, an art show, or a service day). Pair board members with donors for pre- and post-conversation. Your mission in action becomes a natural focus for interaction. It breaks the ice and it's uplifting. For example, Resources for the Future (RFF) sponsors lectures around the country where its staff presents new research findings.

> *Providing a structure to a board member's engagement in fundraising is critical. If a board member has someone whom she'd like to introduce to your organization, she needs to know where to take that person. Creating an introductory activity to your organization, like a luncheon or a tour, gives board members something concrete that they can offer. — Mark Hierholzer, consultant and former executive director*

Piggybacking on these events, the development staff will plan a pre- or post-lecture reception or dinner and invite prospective donors, board members, and other leaders in the field. Says RFF Vice President of Development Lea Harvey, "I have found that having our board members in the room with our leading researchers and with donors or prospects is one of the highest impact things that I can orchestrate because it combines what we do as an organization with the prestige of our board leadership. It's about creating an environment where people can feed off of each other's enthusiasm, where there is an opportunity for an excitement to build. And it's easy and natural for board members, because it's just asking them to be involved in inspiring moments where chemistry can be created. They just have to show up and be themselves."

These two resources can give you more ideas about how to create donor cultivation events:

- *FriendRaising* by Hildy Gottlieb. Gottlieb suggests that nonprofits create a "Community Engagement/Friendraising" plan that is "part fundraising, part marketing" to help identify and cultivate supporters in the community who will help advance the organization in a variety of ways.[vi] Her book includes dozens of ideas, such as tours, house parties, and focus groups, which board members can host, invite guests to, or simply attend to get to know potential donors.

- *The Point of Entry Handbook* by Terry Axelrod. Axelrod is pioneer of The Benevon Model®,[vii] a fundraising program for building life-long donors. A key component of the model is what Axelrod calls the Point of Entry® event — an event that introduces a potential donor to your organization and that serves as the starting point of the donor relationship-building process. In her book, Axelrod describes a variety of ways to hold a Point of Entry® event and how to make them most effective.

Create a campaign. Many fundraisers note that it's often easiest to engage board members in a capital campaign because capital campaigns have clear structures for how board members are involved and the time frame required. Bring the benefits of the capital campaign structure to your annual fundraising efforts. Says former National Vice President for Development at Volunteers of America Kathleen Rae King, "The formality of a campaign creates excitement and provides structure and a clear timeframe — a beginning and an end. You can create a campaign around an event, around a newly launched strategic plan, or you can hold your annual giving program as a campaign and cap it with an event." Adds Cleveland Museum of Art Deputy Director and Chief Advancement Officer August Napoli, "Campaigns galvanize a board around a goal and keep trustees on task. The process of planning for a campaign forces trustees to be more laser focused on the institution than they normally would be because there is urgency to a campaign. I think an organization should always be in a campaign or one stage of it. If the needs aren't there for a capital campaign, you can look at your annual fund in the same way as a campaign."

To learn how one nonprofit, Miriam's Kitchen, created a campaign structure to better engage its board, see Case Study #2 on page 53.

CASE STUDY #1

Board Members of Volunteers of America of North Louisiana Advance the Donor Relationship-Building Process

The fundraising program of Volunteers of America of North Louisiana (VOA-NL), which it calls "Cherish the Children", is a major donor program that it started 11 years ago, based on the Benevon Model® (see page 51). The model relies on building personal relationships with individuals to create lifelong donors for the organization. The relationship process begins with introductory events — bimonthly tours of VOA-NL program sites. The tours, hosted by a board member, give guests an up-close view of the mission of VOA-NL and the impact it is having in the community. VOA-NL also takes the introductory events "on the road" by doing presentations at outside venues, such as a board member's church. Tour guests are invited by board members, staff, volunteers and other donors.

Once an individual has attended a tour, VOA-NL staff follows up to find out if and how that individual would like to get involved. This is part of an ongoing cultivation effort with everyone who attends a tour. Says VOA-NL Vice President of Communications and Development Lisa Brandeburg, "I call every tour guest the day after the tour and thank them for coming. I don't ask them to do anything, but I want to hear what they saw, what they heard, and just really listen. I gauge their level of enthusiasm and ask if they would like to get involved. Most of the time people do." Based on the results of that conversation, Lisa and other staff reach out to the tour guests throughout the year, informing them of volunteer opportunities and providing updates on VOA-NL's work, all as part of the cultivation process.

The tours and the follow-up cultivation culminate in VOA-NL's annual Cherish the Children Breakfast, a free, one-hour event where VOA-NL talks about its accomplishments and needs, and asks guests for a multi-year donation. It's the only "ask" that VOA-NL makes during the year. Everyone who has attended a tour during the year is invited to the breakfast, as well as current donors, volunteers, and friends of board and staff. Says Lisa, "We don't keep it a secret that it is a fundraising event, but there are no expectations; we don't want to strong-arm anyone." She says that in recent years, about 850 people attend the event, and that about half of the guests make a donation.

VOA-NL's fundraising model provides a number of ways for board members to be involved. Board members are asked to support the Cherish the Children program in at least one of the following ways:

· Ensuring that at least 15 people whom the board member invites attend a tour
· Arranging a tour "on the road" with a local group, like a church group or fraternal society
· Serving as a board greeter for at least one tour
· Serving as a table captain at the breakfast event

Because the Cherish the Children program relies heavily on personal contact with donors, VOA-NL also asks board members to make phone calls to donors to thank them for their donation and to invite donors to special events and programs.

Says Lisa, "Before this model, I can't even remember how we involved our board. Now that our model is so systematic, every board member is involved. We've taken the fear off the table, because this model is very respectful of people, and lets them choose what they want to do. All we are asking of board members is to invite their friends to come learn about an organization that they themselves love, and the rest is up to that individual."

CASE STUDY #2
How Miriam's Kitchen Developed a Campaign to Structure its Board's Participation in Fundraising

Miriam's Kitchen, a Washington, DC-based nonprofit that works to end chronic homelessness, raises funds in a variety of ways: from individuals (small and large gifts), corporate sponsors, foundations, workplace giving, and special events. Parts of its fundraising model (such as foundation grants and workplace giving) are almost entirely staff driven, but others parts rely on board members, such as identifying and cultivating major gift donors (individuals and corporations) and identifying guests and corporate sponsors for the organization's annual gala dinner and auction, "100 Bowls of Compassion".

A few years ago, at the urging of board members, Miriam Kitchen's Chief Development and Communications Officer Sara Gibson worked with the chief executive and board to create a board campaign as a way of providing a structure in which board members could conduct their fundraising. Says Sara, "Many of our board members come from the corporate world, and a few years ago one of these board members said to us, 'We can't fundraise in the fourth quarter, it's too busy; let's do the fundraising in the first quarter of the year and run it as a sales cycle.' So we created a campaign, because it's similar to what our board members do in their own companies and they are familiar with it. In 2012, we held a campaign from the end of January to mid-April, which culminated nicely with our gala in May, a focal point for much of our fundraising."

As part of its structure, and also at the request of board members, the board campaign had its own fundraising goal. Says Sara, "Instead of just saying to the board, 'We as an organization need to raise $3,000,000 this year,' we also say, 'and $300,000 is the goal that we'd like your direct help with.' It makes it more tangible, because $3,000,000 can feel too big, and no number is not specific enough."

Because of the compressed timeframe of the board campaign and the immediacy of the May gala, the Miriam's Kitchen board campaign follows a tight structure that includes training and preparation, kickoff, and weekly check-in calls and e-mails. Board members focus on identifying and making calls on potential corporate sponsors of the gala, establishing other corporate contacts for the organization, and inviting guests to the gala. Says Sara, "The Miriam's Kitchen board is most effective when it is focused. We have found success in providing the board with specifics in terms of goals, metrics, and structure. And because we get to know our board members individually, we can help them find ways and provide support so that they each can be successful."

Package your "ask" so board members can "sell." It's well-known in the business world that the way a product is packaged helps to sell it. This is true in the nonprofit world as well. Packaging your request for funding in a compelling and easy-to-deliver way makes it easier for a board member to pick it up and run with it. For example, Cristo Rey Jesuit High School, a private school for inner-city high school students in Baltimore, raises funds to subsidize its annual operating costs so that it can keep its tuition fees affordable to lower income families. Instead of asking for donations to support "general operating costs" of the school, the school calculates its operating costs on a per pupil basis and packages the request as a scholarship. Says Rev. John W. Swope, S.J., president of Cristo Rey Jesuit, "Too often, nonprofit staff members think like insiders. We know we need to fund the operations of the school, so we ask for a gift for operations to fund items like salaries or the electricity. But asking for a gift for operations does not generate excitement. Here's what is exciting — by funding those things, donors can transform the lives of students! So at Cristo Rey Jesuit, we ask for a scholarship gift, so that donors can more clearly see how their gift, which funds our operating costs, is transforming the life of an individual child."

Vice President for Resource Development Denise Nelson, discussing her experience at Habitat for Humanity, says "We created sponsorship packages for individuals and corporations to make it easy for board members to sell. For example, you could sponsor the full cost of building a home at $100,000. It was an entire package — a 'home sponsor' could send a group of volunteers from his or her company, church, or organization to work on the building project. They received name recognition, and we provided team building exercises for the volunteers — it was all part of the package. We also had packages at other levels — $50,000, $10,000, and $5,000 — so the packages worked for individuals and companies with a range of giving capacities. We gave board members the full menu of sponsorship opportunities so they had flexibility to decide what to ask for and from whom. It made the board members feel more comfortable, and a lot of board members who were not able to

DEFINE SUCCESS FOR THE FUNDRAISING PROCESS

Part of good structure is having clear parameters for success. We usually communicate clearly to board members the financial goals of our fundraising campaign. But when it comes to framing what success looks like as part of the fundraising process, we sometimes leave out some key facts. We as development staff know that it takes many "nos" before we get to a 'yes' when asking for a financial gift of support. But this may not be as obvious to board members. Setting expectations early about likely results around fundraising helps to manage board members' feelings of success or failure. Says Potomac Conservancy President Hedrick Belin, "You want board members' experiences to be fun and rewarding, and fundraising inherently has this risk of rejection and discomfort. So it's important to help board members understand what success in fundraising looks like. I like to say that fundraising is a lot like batting in baseball. When you get up to the plate and you get a hit one out of three times — a .333 batting average — that's considered success, and you'll advance to the next level. But that means you've failed 66.6 percent of the time, which in places like our academic system is a big fail! But in fundraising, that's success. So you need to rejigger the expectations of board members."

Some organizations find it helpful to define board member success in fundraising in terms of their participation in relationship-building activities. Says National Conference on Citizenship Executive Director Ilir Zherka, "I tell board members that as long as they are building relationships, they are advancing our fundraising efforts. The relationships produce donations, because people are inspired to give when they like what you are doing and they feel a part of your cause. We had one board member who had a house party, and he was really frustrated because out of the 30 people there, only one person became a donor. But, that person went on to join the board, and gave lots of money himself, and then turned around and invited other people. And then he did a lot of dinners and lunches, and I could tell that he was frustrated that most people whom he invited did not turn around and give us money. I would remind him that he was one out of 30 at that initial house party, and that was okay. You never know where or when that relationship is going to blossom into a funder relationship."

Reinforce the importance of relationship-building activities by reporting and recognizing those activities during your board meetings. At Volunteers of America of North Louisiana, board members are asked to be involved in the fundraising program by inviting guests to VOA-NL agency tours and being a table captain at the annual breakfast (see Case Study #1 on page 52). And those are the same measures that show up at the VOA-NL board meetings — the number of guests attending tours and the number of board member table captains. Says VOA-NL Vice President Lisa Brandeburg, "We want to make sure that there is a consistency with what we are asking board members to do and what we are reporting on in our meetings. This also helps deepen their understanding of our fundraising model."

CHAPTER 6

SUPPORT BOARD MEMBERS EVERY STEP OF THE WAY

Once your board members have the motivation, context, and structure for engaging in fundraising, they are ready to take on fundraising tasks. Our role as staff continues to be important at this stage, because board member follow-through depends largely on staff support. As staff, it's important to recognize the distinct aspects of each step in the fundraising process and offer training and support to board members so that they can carry out their responsibilities successfully.

Key to supporting board members with their fundraising tasks is mastering the art of "managing up"[viii] — managing individuals at a higher level of authority. In her book *Managing Up*, Rosanne Badowski, who served as executive assistant to GE's Jack Welch for 14 years, says that managing up is "first and foremost the art of saving time for those above you and helping them to prioritize in the face of almost overwhelming demands on their time and attention." With board members and fundraising, this means helping them with their fundraising tasks where we can, providing timely reminders, and creating "triggers" to encourage action — all with an attitude that embodies friendliness, diplomacy, and respect.

> I like to think of good staff work as being like a dance with board members, which I call 'lead and follow.' What it means is that the staff needs to need to get out in front of board members and set the stage for board members to be successful. Then staff gets out of the way and follows them through and supports them so they are successful. Board members can't mobilize themselves, so you have to get out in front of them, set the stage so that they can be successful, get out of the way so that they can do their work, then get back out there and set the stage on the next issue. — Matthew Downey, program director, nonprofit services, Grand Valley State University

Not surprisingly, board members want, need, and expect good support. Says Sara Gibson, chief development and communications officer of Miriam's Kitchen, who also serves as a board member for another nonprofit organization, "Board members need to be managed, and I say that *as a board member*. If someone doesn't nudge me, I will not do it. Even if I'm more skilled at fundraising than other board members, I still expect to be managed. I have found that the more senior people are, the more they accept and expect help from staff. In my role as chief development officer, I say to board members, 'Let me just clarify that what I'm hearing you say is, you want me to bug you?' And they say, 'Yes!'"

HELP BOARD MEMBERS GET THE JOB DONE

What does good staff support look like? Listed below are ways to support board members with their fundraising responsibilities.

Assist with tasks. Most tasks have several component steps. For example, asking a board member to invite a friend or colleague to an open house includes identifying the friend, composing the e-mail, acquiring the e-mail address, sending the e-mail, and following up to see if the friend can attend. Several of those steps can be done by the staff, such as composing a draft e-mail or doing the follow-up.

When you ask board members to do a particular task, let them know which pieces you as staff can do or can help them with. Says Cleveland Museum of Art Deputy Director and Chief Advancement Officer August Napoli, "Once the board member has agreed to his role, you start drilling down into the specific components and say, 'Of this, what part can I do productively for you?' You can't just say, 'Here are five prospects, go get them!' or 'Here's a dandy proposal and folder; let me know when you are finished.' That's not helping them at all. Rather you say, 'Allow me to make the appointment.' And then you call the prospect and it goes something like this: 'Tom asked me to call you to see if we can set up a meeting.' 'What does Tom want to talk about?' 'Well, we have this campaign going on…' and so forth. So by the time you and Tom meet the donor, the donor knows that he is going to be asked for a donation, or he wouldn't have agreed to the meeting. So the staff is essentially doing most of the work."

> My philosophy is to do EVERYTHING for the board member, everything! The thing that I give the most emphasis to is the need to support the board. I think a lot of staff assumes that because this person has joined the board, they will take the initiative. And it took me joining a board to realize that this is not how it works. So, for example, for our Jamboree event, I will say to a board member, 'I remember that you said you thought these people would enjoy the Jamboree; well, it's coming up, and here's a template e-mail for an invitation to the Jamboree that you can use.'
> — Amy Nakamoto, executive director, DC SCORES

In addition to breaking tasks into specific steps, limit the number of steps you ask a board member to take on. The goal is for them to be successful, so keep it simple, e.g., two or three steps, not 10. As Lakeland College Vice President for Advancement, Strategy, and Innovation Ken Strmiska says, "Board members are busy, and if you give them a complicated task, they'll often say, 'I just can't take it, my life is too full.' So as development staff, we have to say, 'Look, here's the piece I need you to do,' and make sure it is well defined and easy to do."

For two tools that you can use to help board members with their fundraising tasks, see Tool #5 and Tool #6 on pages 84 and 85 of the Board Fundraising Toolbox.

Board Fundraising Tool #5 & #6

Create triggers to spur action. Everyone benefits from having goals and deadlines to stimulate action. Your fundraising program itself may contain natural deadlines associated with events and activities such as a gala, a house party, a tour, or a service project. You can also create "triggers" that move board members to action. For example, during a fundraising campaign at the Friends Committee on National Legislation, Associate Executive Secretary Jim Cason scheduled biweekly conference calls for board members on the campaign committee. During these calls, board members reported their progress, asked questions, and received feedback. Says Jim, "The occasion of the calls became a deadline for board members to make their 'asks,' since during the call people reported on what they had accomplished. The calls were a great way for people to share what was working and exchange ideas, but they were equally valuable as a stimulus for action."

Keep in touch. Board members lead busy lives and have many competing demands on their time. Friendly and respectful reminders help board members complete their tasks. You can ask your board member, "If I haven't heard from you by (date), is it OK if I call you?" or "When would you like me to check in with you to see how things are going?" Says Jane O'Connell, president of the Altman Foundation and a board member of another organization, "Board members often get criticized for not following through on a task, and it's not that they are not willing, but board members have other lives. Directors of development need to realize that board members need materials and crutches to do what they are doing. I've got something on my desk right now — I'm supposed to write a letter to someone, and there's a wonderful development director who has reminded me three times. I'm not going to forget about it, because she's not going to let me forget. She's perfectly nice about it. She's not being a pest."

In addition to providing reminders, regular fundraising progress reports and updates are a helpful motivator. Silence can be interpreted as a lack of interest or importance, and inactivity by the board is a natural consequence. On the other hand, a proactive board communication strategy pays off in both time and interest. Says DC SCORES Executive Director Amy Nakamoto, "By not communicating regularly, it makes the time when you do communicate much harder, because you have to reorient, reengage, remotivate, and recontextualize. You don't want to have to provide 10 months of backstory. Instead, you want to create an environment where you can just pick up the phone and ask a board member for advice."

Provide tools. Arm your board members with the right kinds of messaging tools, such as key talking points and stories that illustrate impact, to empower them to talk about your organization in a clear and compelling way. Says Tahirih Justice Center Executive Director Layli Miller-Muro, "Right now, we are working on comprehensive immigration reform. It would not be reasonable to have every board member understand each nuance of the legislation, but they should have the top five talking points that illustrate Tahirih's position on immigration reform. So every quarter I provide them with an executive summary report that includes those highlights."

When people are busy, their attention spans can be short, and volunteer board members are no exception.

(Our executive director) Craig has an iron-clad rule that, for significant news, the board will always hear it first. For example, we had a big event Monday night, and the morning after we were sending out some talking points to the media about the success of the event, and Craig asked, 'When is this going out?', and the communications manager said 'In about 30 minutes,' and Craig said, 'Good, in 15 minutes I want you to send this out to the board, because I don't want them to see a blog about us that they haven't already heard.' — Patricia Cornell, director of development, Food & Friends

One of our board members agreed to send a $2,500 request for support to a colleague of his who was a property manager. I drafted the letter for him, so all he needed to do was to print the letter on his letterhead and sign it. Several times he came to me and said he didn't have the letter, and even though I knew I had sent it to him, I happily resent it. It took four months for him to get the letter out. We actually had given up hope on this effort. And then one day, a check for $10,000 came in the mail from the property manager. For me the lesson was, you sometimes have to keep doing things over and over again. In this case, it was what the board member needed. — Jennifer Hoffman, deputy director, Prince George's Child Resource Center

Keep board communiqués brief — one-to-two-page memos in bullet point format — to help them focus on key points. Videos are also effective. They are increasingly easy to make and share, and can allow accompanying written materials to be brief and focused.

Also, furnish board members with "cultivation tools" that they can share with friends to highlight the work that your organization does. A news clipping, a press release, or a research paper highlights your organization's accomplishments and is easy to pass along. Director of Development John Westfall-Kwong of Lambda Legal says, "During the holiday season, we send board members a weekly fundraising message that they can personalize and send to their network of cultivation assignments. This provides them with a tool to share so that they don't have to write an e-mail themselves."

> Most of us who go into this as volunteers are somewhat motivated initially, but it makes a tremendous difference to have a staff person who truly follows through and continually pushes you to do the next step. Some of us need more pushing at times than others. I have found that when we had to keep our fellow board members motivated and moving, the way to do that was to keep in touch with them, and the staff person pushed me, and we then pushed the board members. — Charlotte Berry, board member, United Way Association of South Carolina

Encourage peer support. Look for opportunities to engage your board development committee or other successful board fundraisers in supporting fellow members with fundraising tasks. Says Food & Friends Executive Director Craig Shniderman, "We've been successful at using board members who are the most effective fundraisers to be the guides and encouragers of other fellow board members. Everybody knows that my director of development and I raise money for a living, so our credibility is less when we say, 'You can do this.' It's like a neurosurgeon saying to you, 'You can do a heart transplant, I do them all the time, it's not that hard.' You'd say, 'Well, yes, you are a surgeon!' But if you have a board member coaching another board member about a fundraising activity, saying, 'Look, if I did it, you can do it,' or 'It's not as hard as it seems,' that message is more effective, because the board member is not regarded as an expert or professional; she is a peer."

If you ask your successful board fundraisers to provide coaching or follow-up assistance to their colleagues, good staff support is still important. The need for staff involvement doesn't lessen; rather, the focus shifts from providing direct support to board members on the front line to helping board members who are coaching their colleagues.

PROVIDE FORMAL AND INFORMAL TRAINING

Training is another important way to support board members in carrying out their fundraising responsibilities effectively. Training strengthens a board member's skills, confidence, and comfort level. To ensure that board members get the most out of fundraising training, we need to be thoughtful and intentional in our approach, with a special focus on furnishing appropriate context and follow-through. Some board members may resist the notion of being trained or feel it's a waste of their time. Says Jane O'Connell, president of the Altman Foundation and a board member of another organization, "In some cases, for some boards, training can be very helpful. But I can think of some boards where training wouldn't work, at least not a formal training. Some board members feel they don't need training; they believe they know it already. So then you have to figure out another way to deliver the information."

Determining appropriate board training and education is not the staff's task alone. Engage your board members in a discussion about what kind of training they will benefit from and how and when it can be most effectively delivered. This is a great topic to bring to your board fundraising committee or to your governance committee as part of a larger conversation on continuing board education. As with other aspects of board service, board members will be more receptive to fundraising training and education, especially the more formal variety, when it is initiated by their peers.

Training is most effective when it is more than just a one-time event but rather a series of learning opportunities. An ongoing set of experiences over time is best for strengthening your board members' knowledge and comfort level for fundraising. As fundraising consultant Andrea Kihlstedt states, "People learn best when they learn in small bits and then have a chance to practice and learn something more."[ix] A presentation or workshop can be one component of training, but there are many ways that training and education can be offered in less formal ways — through conversations, board discussions, shadowing assignments, pairing less experienced board members with those more experienced, debriefings, coaching, and stories from others about their personal experiences.

Position training for success. Training needs to be focused and intentional. It should be offered just as board members are getting ready to embark on fundraising activities. A lengthy gap between acquisition of new knowledge and skills and the application of them can undermine the learnings and sap energy.

Training that doesn't have a good context for the board member can be unproductive. Says former National Vice President for Development at Volunteers of America Kathleen Rae King, "It's best to have training that is linked to a particular activity that board members are being asked to do in the near future."

Training will be more productive after an initial framing. Through framing, we share with our boards the background and context on the organization and its fundraising program, and the role they are being asked to play (see Chapter 3). Says consultant Debbie Hechinger, "Just because the organization has decided to go into a fundraising mode doesn't mean it's time to start introducing all of the training and education about fundraising to the board, because there can be a high resistance to doing it." The label of "training" connotes that you are preparing someone to do something, and for that you need prior buy-in. Well-executed framing can help.

It's also important to determine who needs what type of training. For example, provide role playing training on "making the ask" only to those board members who will be doing solicitations, or talk with them individually about what to say. Says consultant Betsy Garside, "Sometimes training can tread a very fine line between being useful and patronizing. I had a very helpful role-playing interaction with the principal of a private school on whose board I served, and the role playing was helpful for me because it was a spur of the moment, one-on-one interaction. It didn't feel like something I had been set up for. And, it hit me at just the right moment. I was going to have to make an ask in the next few days."

Enlist outside help. While many executive directors and development directors have the knowledge and skill set to lead a training session, they may not always be the best ones to do so. As consultant Chuck Loring says, "Many executive directors and development staff don't have the credibility to deliver the training to the board because they are perceived as having a vested interest in the outcome. An outside expert can sometimes be more successful because they are considered to be a more neutral party."

Hiring a consultant is one option, but there are others. Ask a board or staff member from another nonprofit organization to lead a fundraising presentation with your board. Or, invite a team of board members to join you at a public training program offered by a local nonprofit management support organization, community foundation, or university.

Invest in conversations. Training and education can take place in the course of a conversation with a board member, although it takes some forethought. Grand Teton National Park Foundation President Leslie Mattson uses conversations with her board members as an opportunity for training and role-playing. "When I am having a one-on-one conversation with a board member about their prospects and how to approach them, I might say, 'If I were having the conversation with so-and-so, this is what I might say,' or 'If I were making the call, this is how I'd handle it.' So it comes out in a conversational sort of way that doesn't feel like training." Consultant Debbie Hechinger also advocates using conversations as opportunities for education, "Every time an executive director communicates with a board member, there is an opportunity for education. One way to use conversation as a means for helping board members surmount the hurdle in fundraising is to ask them to help you think through the best way to handle a situation — whether that situation is a call to an individual donor, a conversation with a foundation officer, or a meeting with a corporate giving advisor. In explaining the situation at hand, you can use problem solving as a way to educate the board member and build his or her confidence at the same time."

Board meetings are another venue for learning through thoughtful reporting and purposeful conversation. Says Cleveland Museum of Art Deputy Director and Chief Advancement Officer August Napoli, "I find success not in 'teaching' board members, but in framing my development reports in a way that is educational as well as informative. For example, our success at converting major donor prospects to actual donors is typically 30 to 50 percent. So I frame every prospect report for the board by saying that it's still a win if 30 percent of prospects make a donation, or, if we ask for $1 million and we get 30 percent, that's not a loss, that's a win. And I present this in tone and decorum and posture like, 'Of course you know this already, but let me share this with you.'"

Real examples of a fundraising ask, when shared by a board colleague, can both demystify the experience for others and reinforce behavior by modeling it. When part of a board meeting, shared stories can be engaging and motivating, particularly when followed by an open Q&A format to encourage participation. Dan McQuaid, CEO of One OC, has used this technique with boards and says, "In psychology, anticipatory behavior is how to help people deal with anxiety. Role playing, illustration, and case examples are great ways to do that. When you are in a board meeting, and you have a board member who has successfully been able to introduce the organization to a new potential supporter, have that individual tell her story of what she did and how she did it. I ask questions like, 'How did that happen, what did you do, what made it work, how did you feel about it?' It's helpful to ask about the feelings, because a board member might say, 'Well, I was a little bit nervous since I do business with these folks.' That's good to have out there, because it gets those fears out on the table and can lead to a productive discussion."

First-person stories don't necessarily need to be limited to your own board members; you also can bring in board members from a similar organization for their remarks. Or, invite donors who are willing to share their perspective on being asked and how they decide to give.

Team up for success. New board members not as familiar with the organization may have a steeper climb for fundraising success. You can accelerate their learning by pairing them with seasoned board members. They can observe, learn, and experience early accomplishment. Says Elizabeth Costas, executive director of The Frances L. and Edwin L. Cummings Memorial Fund, "I once served on a committee where we interviewed potential board candidates, and another committee member joined me who was new to this. He was very nervous initially, but afterwards he was quite enthusiastic and said the experience was very helpful." An inexperienced board member also might accompany the executive director or development director on a cultivation visit or on an ask (depending on the donor) to observe or to share their own enthusiasm for the organization's work.

Even if two board members have a similar level of experience, it can still be helpful to pair them together for a fundraising assignment. Says Dan McQuaid, CEO of One OC, "People become a lot bolder and learn more quickly when they work with others rather than by themselves. It can give them courage to take steps that they otherwise might feel apprehensive about. It also provides them someone with whom to do pre-meeting rehearsal and post-meeting assessment."

However you decide to structure training and education for your board, it's helpful to remember that there's nothing like on-the-job experience for really understanding how to carry out fundraising activities. The 70:20:10 Model of the Center for Creative Leadership[x] states that about 70 percent of learning comes from on-the-job experiences, tasks, and problem solving; 20 percent from feedback and coaching; and about 10 percent from training courses and reading. Training and education are critical for providing a solid baseline of understanding, but there's nothing like getting one's feet wet for real learning to sink in.

RECOGNIZE AND THANK

Just as it's critical to be good stewards of donors, it's also important to be good stewards of board members. This includes thanking them at every step along the way, but also providing them with ongoing encouragement and recognition. It also means taking time to celebrate accomplishments.

Sometimes we underestimate how meaningful our own thank you can be to a board member, especially when the power differential between staff and board is pronounced. Says consultant Carol Weisman, "Early in my volunteer career, I received a note from a development director with an organization on whose board I served, and it said, 'Carol, I don't know what we would have done without you. The way you handled that situation was brilliant. We are going to take you with us on every call!' Well, I just blew up like a big blowfish! Even though we had different roles within the organization, their kind words really meant the world to me."

Express specific gratitude.
A thank you is more powerful when it is specific. Consider the difference between saying, "Thank you for your help," and "Thank you for attending the reception and talking with so many of our donors. You really took the time to get to know them, and I could tell they were quite moved by your personal story of our mission." By elaborating the reason for your gratitude, you reinforce the behavior you hope will be replicated.

Recognize accomplishments.
Most people like to be recognized by their peers, and it can be an important modeling opportunity for other board members to learn from. Says Food & Friends Director of Development Patricia Cornell, "In board meetings, I recognize a few board members who have successfully solicited or identified a new donor, and I'll ask them to share what they did. So they might say, 'I got the president of such and such bank to come to Food & Friends for a tour and lunch' or 'I went with the executive director to ask a major donor for $75,000.'

I think this has been useful, because the board members all know that no one is chomping

As part of a capital campaign, we took a group of donors on a director-led museum tour followed by dinner. One of our trustees, "John Smith," had agreed to speak at the dinner about his own gift to the campaign and why he thought it was important. After the dinner, I thanked everyone for coming, and said, "As you know, we are concluding our capital campaign, and John Smith from our board and his wife wanted to be with us tonight to say a few words." So John and his wife came to the podium and started talking about why they decided to support the campaign. They spoke from the heart about why they gave. Then I wrapped up the evening by providing everyone with a packet of information and a request for support, and let them know that we would follow up with them in a few days.

A few weeks later, a person who had attended the event, and whom we had targeted for a $100,000 gift, turned around and gave us a $1 million contribution! I immediately picked up the phone and called John Smith and told him the great news, and said "I know that the comments that you and Sally made really made the difference." And I wasn't stretching the truth, they did!

At the next board meeting, I told this story to our full board and thanked John for sharing his passion and inspiring others. After the meeting, three board members approached me to say that they would be happy to talk at a future event if we needed them. You talk about motivation — that's motivation!

at the bit to go out and do these things, but when they see others doing it, they say, 'If you can do it, I can do it.'"

Share final results. Sometimes the outcome of a board member's cultivation efforts isn't known immediately — it can take months, sometimes years, to nurture a major donor. Investing in a good donor database system will allow you to more easily track the outcomes of board member efforts. For example, if board members are involved in thanking donors for a recent gift, let them know when those donors give the next gift and the amount of the gift. Or, share with board members the retention rate of donors who have been thanked personally by them versus those who have received a standard thank-you letter. This reinforces the value of board member involvement. At Catholic Charities Ft. Worth (CCFW), one of the ways board members assist in fundraising is by inviting people on an introductory tour of the organization. When thanking board members for their help with this, the staff shows the board the average size gift received by someone who has been on a tour (around $3,000) compared to the average size gift of someone who has not been on a tour (around $150). Says CCFW CEO Heather Reynolds, "By sharing this data, we not only thank them but we show them the impact that they are having on this organization." For more about how to involve board members in personally thanking donors, see Tool #7 in the Board Fundraising Toolbox on page 86.

Board Fundraising Tool #7

Recognize all efforts. While it's helpful to share positive results when you have them, be sure you also thank board members individually for effort and actions, not just results. It takes a lot of outreach to many people to find those who will support your organization, so recognize all of the actions taken, invitations sent, and contacts made on the part of board members, not just the ones that result in a contribution.

Also recognize any role that a board member may have played in cultivating a donor. Says Cleveland Museum of Art Deputy Director and Chief Advancement Officer August Napoli, "If John Doe decides to make his gift, and a trustee did something, *anything*, to cultivate Mr. Doe, we give the trustee credit for bringing that gift to closure. We want trustees to see themselves as part of the team that made that gift happen."

Make recognition a habit. Incorporate practices for regularly thanking and recognizing board members. It can be as simple as designating the first day of the month or every other Friday as the day you send out an e-mail to recognize all board fundraising activity. Or, create a board member newsletter or a regular progress report that includes a section for thanking and recognizing board members. Consultant Carol Weisman recounts an effective tool used by a friend. "Every Friday my friend sent out an informal e-mail that she called *The Good News Gazette*. It was a maximum of two paragraphs, and the subject line would say something like, 'Special Thanks to Kathy and Patrick.' The e-mail would say things like, 'Kathy got us into Build-a-Bear Workshop and we're having a meeting with the CEO. Does anyone else know the CEO Maxine Clark?' The e-mail recognized board members, and it sometimes also included a specific request for some additional assistance, right at the moment it was needed."

Set up early wins. Thanking board members and giving them positive feedback is so important that when board members are first starting to assist with fundraising, look for ways you can set them up for early wins. Says Elizabeth Costas, executive director of The Frances L. and Edwin L. Cummings Memorial Fund, "Explore how you can make people feel successful upfront. Success breeds excitement, so start with some of the easier assignments where success is more likely, and then build up to the more difficult assignments."

CONCLUSION

A key premise of this book is that if you want to get more out of your board, invest in the staff that supports the board. Board members have wisdom, experience, skills, contacts, and diverse viewpoints to offer, but they also have myriad other obligations that compete for their attention. By working collaboratively with them, a savvy executive director or development director can capitalize on the assets board members offer.

While it takes time to support and manage board members, it also takes an openness and willingness to seek out and understand their perspectives. We as development staff have long been encouraged to put ourselves in the shoes of donors, to see the world through their eyes. This book advocates for treating our board members in a similar way. By getting to know them well, and supporting them well, we are creating influential ambassadors for wider organizational success.

> At the end of the day, we're asking board members to provide their intellectual capital, introductions, access and "asks" to people in their networks, and it is their reputations at stake. They worked very hard to build their reputations over the years. So in that light, the nonprofit staff has the responsibility to use their board assets wisely, and with care.
> — Joseph Suarez, executive advisor, community partnerships, Booz Allen Hamilton

The ideas and advice in this book are not intended as must-do's, but rather as a set of possibilities that you can evaluate based on what makes sense for your board and your organization right now. Be realistic about what you can do, and what you hope to gain, from your board's involvement in fundraising. Nonprofits often operate under constrained conditions, trying to do a lot with limited resources. Involving the board in fundraising can take a considerable amount of staff time and energy, but can yield equally large payoffs if we are deliberate in our investment.

By articulating what successful board engagement looks like for your organization, you are more likely to meet with success and discover a sense of accomplishment that all can share in. Rather than trying to do too much too quickly, start with achievable goals and a manageable mandate, and grow from there. The self-motivation that your board members will experience from your skillful facilitation and some early success can be a powerful catalyst that propels them to do more. Onward!

REFERENCES AND RECOMMENDED READING

Beyond Fundraising: New Strategies for Nonprofit Innovation and Investment, Second Edition by Kay Sprinkel Grace, Wiley, 2011.

Boards That Love Fundraising: A How-to Guide for Your Board by Robert Zimmerman and Ann Lehman, John Wiley & Sons, 2004.

BoardSource Nonprofit Governance Index 2012, BoardSource, 2012.

The Benevon Model for Sustainable Funding: A Step-by-Step Guide to Getting it Right by Terry Axelrod, Benevon Publications, 2012.

Development Committee by Eugene Tempel, BoardSource, 2004.

Donor Centered Leadership by Penelope Burk, Cygnus Applied Research, 2013.

Fearless Fundraising for Nonprofit Boards, Second Edition by Dave Sternberg, BoardSource, 2008.

"Finding Your Funding Model" by Peter Kim, Gail Perreault, and William Foster, *Stanford Social Innovation Review*, Fall 2011.

Fired-Up Fundraising: Turn Board Passion into Action by Gail Perry, John Wiley & Sons, 2007.

FriendRaising: Community Engagement Strategies for Boards Who Hate Fundraising but Love Making Friends by Hildy Gottlieb, Renaissance Press, 2006.

Governance as Leadership: Reframing the Work of Nonprofit Boards by Richard P. Chait, William P. Ryan, and Barbara E. Taylor, John Wiley & Son, 2005.

Managing Up: How to Forge an Effective Relationship with Those Above You by Rosanne Badowski, Crown Business, 2003.

Nonprofit Sustainability: Making Strategic Decisions for Financial Viability by Jeanne Bell, Jan Masaoka, and Steve Zimmerman, Jossey Bass, 2010.

Raising More Money – The Point of Entry Handbook by Terry Axelrod, Raising More Money Publications, 2005.

Special Report: Engaging Board Members in Fundraising, Nonprofit Research Collaborative, 2012.

Ten Basic Responsibilities of Nonprofit Boards by Richard T. Ingram, BoardSource, 2009.

Ten Basic Responsibilities of Nonprofit Boards: The Companion Workbook, BoardSource, 2011.

"Ten Nonprofit Funding Models" by William Foster, Peter Kim, and Barbara Christiansen, *Stanford Social Innovation Review*, Spring 2009.

UnderDeveloped: A National Study of Challenges Facing Nonprofit Fundraising by Jeanne Bell and Marla Cornelius, CompassPoint Nonprofit Services and the Evelyn and Walter Haas, Jr. Fund, San Francisco, CA, 2013.

The Practitioner's Guide to Governance as Leadership: Building High-Performing Nonprofit Boards by Cathy Trower, Jossey Bass, 2013.

Transforming Ordinary People into Fundraising Superheroes…Even Those Who Hate to Ask by Carol Weisman, F.E. Robbins & Sons Press, 2009.

Why We Do What We Do: Understanding Self-Motivation by Edward L. Deci, Penguin Books, 1995.

APPENDIX: BOARD FUNDRAISING TOOLBOX

1. **Board Member Participation in Fund Development at XYZ Organization** (a sample form to use for new and/or prospective board members to let them see the types of fundraising activities that they can engage in as board members with your organization)

2. **New Board Member Get-to-Know-You Questions** (a sample set of questions to ask new or existing board members to get to know them better and enhance their board member experience)

3. **Roles That Board Members Can Play in the Fundraising Process** (a list of roles and related activities that board members can play in the fundraising process)

4. **Examples of Social and Volunteer Opportunities for Board Members** (a sample list of ideas for creating opportunities for board members to get to know each other, the staff, and the organization in a more personal way)

5. **Board Member Network List** (a form that board members can use to focus and stimulate their brainstorming about whom they can introduce to your organization)

6. **Board Member E-mail Invitation Template** (an e-mail invitation template that a board member can customize to send to a friend)

7. **Engaging Board Members in Thanking Donors** (a three-part tool that features ideas and tips on how to organize the program, a sample script for board members to use for their calls, and a sample intake form for board members to use for their calls)

Board Fundraising Tool #1

This is a sample form that you can adapt and share with board members or candidates to educate them about the types of fundraising activities they can engage in as a board member. This is adapted with permission from the nonprofit organization Taxpayers for Common Sense.

BOARD MEMBER PARTICIPATION IN FUND DEVELOPMENT AT XYZ ORGANIZATION

We are delighted that you have chosen to serve as a member of the XYZ Organization Board of Directors! XYZ board members play a key role in advancing the mission of XYZ by ensuring that we have adequate funding for our critical programs and services.

Below is a list of ways that current and past board members have supported XYZ Organization's fund development program. We will call you soon to discuss the best ways for you to get involved!

- **Make a Financial Contribution**
  100 percent board participation signals to donors that the leadership is invested in the success of XYZ. Consider a contribution at a level that is significant for you and consistent with, or greater than, your support for other organizations.

- **Introduce (Executive Director) to Prospective Major Donors or Strategic Contacts**
  Many leaders on the board are already meeting with donors and foundation staff on behalf of their own organizations and interests. There may also be other community or business leaders you know who might be interested in learning more about the work of XYZ. Whenever facilitating a meeting or introduction does not create a conflict of interest, your personal introduction will serve as a strong first impression.

- **Arrange for a Speaking Opportunity for (Executive Director)**
  Many board members have arranged for (executive director) to speak at their place of worship, fraternity club, place of business, and neighborhood association to talk about the important outreach of XYZ.

- **Accompany (Executive Director) on a Major Donor Visit**
  Board members accompany (executive director) on visits with prospective donors — individuals, foundation leaders, and corporate officers. Your presence at a meeting sends an important message that our board members are actively involved in our organization.

- **Serve as a Board Greeter and/or Invite Guests to Attend a Tour of the XYZ Service Center**
  We offer monthly tours of our service center to give community members an up-close view of the services we provide every day. One-hour tours are held the first Monday of the month at 8 a.m..

- **Host a Dinner or Reception in Your Home**
  This can be as small or large, as casual or fancy, as you'd like to make it. The main objective is to introduce new potential supporters to XYZ.

- **I've got another idea! Let's discuss.**

Thank you for your leadership and commitment to XYZ Organization!

Board Fundraising Tool #2

Listed below are questions you can ask new board members (or existing board members) to get to know them better and enhance their board member experience. (This questionnaire includes input from interviews with Nancy Wackstein and Jessica Ziegler of United Neighborhood Houses and Carol Weisman of Board Builders.)

NEW BOARD MEMBER GET-TO-KNOW-YOU QUESTIONS

- What is your connection to (name of organization) and its mission?

- How did you initially discover (name of organization)? Do you have any previous connections with (name of organization) (e.g., as a volunteer, a client, a member, a donor, etc.)?

- What made you decide to join our board as opposed to the boards of other organizations?

- How would you like to contribute to advancing the mission of (name of organization)? Are there particular skills that you would like to use to benefit the organization?

- Are there new skills or experiences you are hoping to gain from your board service?

- Please tell us how we can help you understand (name of organization) more fully as a board member (for example, providing additional information on programs, setting up a site visit, setting up a meeting with other staff or board members).

- Please list ways that you would like to be involved with (name of organization) in the coming year, especially ideas that have not already been discussed.

- What other interest areas, hobbies, or skills would you like to share that you think could be useful to (name of organization)?

- (For board members who have served a year or more) What is your level of satisfaction with your board service with this organization to date?

- What are your initial impressions of (name of organization) — both strengths and areas for improvement?

- What didn't we ask that we should have?

Board Fundraising Tool #3

Listed below are a variety of fundraising activities well suited for board members, grouped by the role that board members play in the fundraising process. Note that only one of the roles involves actually asking for money! Use this form with board members individually or as a group to determine which roles and activities they can take on to advance your organization's fundraising program.

ROLES THAT BOARD MEMBERS CAN PLAY IN THE FUNDRAISING PROCESS

"Inspired Donor" – Board members are first and foremost donors themselves. They do this by

- making an annual gift at the top level of their philanthropy

- offering to make a 2:1 match for funds raised by a group of donors or at a certain level

- making a personal gift and encouraging a group of colleagues to make the same level of gift

"Door Opener" – Board members can introduce their network to the organization, and the organization to their network. They do this by

- providing names of friends and colleagues to invite to a tour or open house of the organization

- introducing the executive director or development director to a personal contact at a foundation or company

- arranging for the executive director to speak to a local group, such as a Rotary Club, place of worship, fraternal society, neighborhood association, or business group

- forwarding a news clipping or press release about the organization to friends and colleagues, along with a comment about their service on the board and an invitation to get involved

- hosting a house party, reception, or social in their home where the executive director or other staff member can speak about the organization's work and impact

- inviting guests to one of the organization's outreach or fundraising events

"**Ambassador**" – Board members engage others in conversation and share information about the organization and its impact. They do this by

- attending events and talking with guests about the organization

- serving as a greeter or host of a tour of your office, project site, or facility

- forwarding a news clipping, press release, or other information about the organization to their network, along with a comment about why they care about the organization

- paying for a guest subscription or membership to your organization for a friend, or paying an event fee for a guest to attend a program sponsored by your organization

"**Validator**" – Board members convey the organization's value to others by virtue of their own support of the organization and its work.[xi] They do this by

- accompanying the executive director or another board member to meet with an individual, company, or foundation

- at a house party or other donor gathering, giving a personal testimony about why they support the organization

- writing a letter to a potential donor about why they support the organization, which can accompany an ask made by the executive director or someone else in the organization

- chair a fundraising campaign of the organization

"**Solicitor**" – Board members ask for support from friends, colleagues, and connections on behalf of the organization. They do this by

- approaching their company's corporate relations department about participating in one of the organization's special events or volunteer projects

- approaching places they do business to ask for a financial or in-kind gift

- asking friends, family, or colleagues to consider making an end-of-year donation to the organization

- telling a prospective donor about why they give to the organization and asking for his or her support

"**Thanker**" – Studies show that thank-you calls from board members influence donors to give again and give more.[xii] Board members can help with thanking donors by

- calling donors within one to three days after the gift has been made to personally thank them

- calling donors six months after the gift has been made to let them know how the organization has been able to put the gift to good use

- signing thank-you letters to donors

- sending hand-written thank-you notes to donors on personal stationery

Board Fundraising Tool #4

Listed below are examples of opportunities for board members, or board and staff members, to get to know each other and the organization better. Adapt these ideas or use them to spark discussion among your own board members. Be sure to pick activities that fit the culture of your organization. (Examples below were provided by nonprofit leaders interviewed for this book, as noted.)

EXAMPLES OF SOCIAL AND VOLUNTEER OPPORTUNITIES FOR BOARD MEMBERS

- I serve on the board of a museum, and we get together socially two to three times a year. Sometimes our get-togethers are museum-related, like an event tied to the opening of an exhibit; other times it's purely social, like cocktails in a board member's home. We also have parties for board members who are rotating off the board, to say thank you. These activities really create a sense of community among the board and the staff. – Jane O'Connell, president, Altman Foundation, board member, Museum of the City of New York and VCG/Governance Matters

- I worked for an environmental organization where the board met annually somewhere in the wilderness, which really got people in the spirit of the organization. One night they would have a campfire for board members. During the campfire, each board member would talk about something that had inspired him or her in the past year. It was a very powerful way for them to learn about each other as people, not just as board members. – Betsy Garside, managing director, Garside Group

- We have social gatherings for board members in people's homes, but we also take on a major project as a board. This year, our board members will be teaching young children how to administer first aid and CPR in their own homes. The socials are important, but the projects build more of a bond. – Charlotte Berry, board member, United Way Association of South Carolina

- We ask board members to participate in a board service activity each year: a Thanksgiving luncheon for clients, which includes preparing the meal and organizing games and activities and/or hosting a game night for clients in one of our housing properties. This builds board camaraderie and helps them understand what we do on the ground every day.
  – Heather Reynolds, president and CEO, Catholic Charities Ft. Worth

- We do two half-day board field trips a year. Since we are all about health of the river and water quality, we might go down to the sewer treatment plant or to restoration projects on the ground, or to meet landowners that have put easements on their properties. – Hedrick Belin, president, Potomac Conservancy

Board Fundraising Tool #5
Adapt and share this form with board members to help them think about the different groups of people they know, and whom they can introduce to your organization. Board members can use this form on their own or as part of a brainstorming meeting with staff or other board members.

BOARD MEMBER NETWORK LIST

Thank you for your willingness to spread the word about the work of (organization name) to your friends and associates! You can use this form to stimulate your thinking about who in your various networks might like to learn more. We will follow up with you to discuss the best ways to reach out to people on your list.

Family Members	
Neighbors	
Work Colleagues / Business Associates / Professional Contacts	
Associates at Places of Worship	
College Buddies / Alumni Groups	
Professional Associates	
Doctor / Dentist / Lawyer / Accountant	
Fraternal Societies / Organizational Memberships and Clubs	
Other Board Service (For Profit or Nonprofit)	

Board Fundraising Tool #6

Below is a sample e-mail that a board member can send to friends or colleagues to invite them to a house party, tour, or some other event to introduce them to your organization. (The nonprofit referenced in this e-mail is fictitious; it is included for illustration purposes only.)

BOARD MEMBER E-MAIL INVITATION TEMPLATE

Dear Veronica,

I think you know that I'm a board member of the nonprofit organization, Families Reading Together. I've been a board member for the past four years, and as you know, it's an organization whose cause — promoting more family reading time together — I'm very passionate about.

Next month, I'm hosting a house party (tour, event) and inviting some of my friends to come and learn more about the work of Families Reading Together and the impact it is having in our area. It would really be terrific if you could come. There will be no pressure on you to make a donation to the organization; in fact, while we wouldn't turn down a gift, that's not the point of the house party. I really see this as an occasion to share the story of what this organization is doing with some of my friends. Whether or not you want to get more involved with Families Reading Together after the house party (tour, event) is up to you.

The house party will take place after work on Friday, October 10, from 5:30pm to 7:30pm, and we'll have hors d'oeuvres and drinks. I do hope you can make it. If you could let me know whether you'll be able to join us by October 3, I'd really appreciate it. Thanks, Veronica.

Best,

Nancy

Board Fundraising Tool #7

Board member thank-you calls to donors can be a rewarding experience for board members, the donors, and the organization. Studies show that donors who receive a personal thank-you call are more likely to make a repeat gift and to increase their next gift.[xiii] Below are some ideas about how to involve your board members in thanking donors.

ENGAGING BOARD MEMBERS IN THANKING DONORS

Ideas and Tips

- **Hold a board "thank-a-thon" at your office.** Invite a group of board members to gather one evening to call donors to thank them for their gift. You may want to hold this right after a fundraising event or campaign, or, you can hold it about six months after the gift was made and frame the calls as both thank-you's and progress updates; in other words, let the donor know how her gift has been used and the impact it's made.

  Kick off the evening with a brief welcome, and share any key information about the calls with your board members. Share sample scripts and any points to cover or key messages for the calls (see sample on next page) but also encourage them to be authentic and talk in a way that is natural for them.

  One of the main benefits of doing donor thank-you calls as a group is that it can be a great team-building event, and it gives board members and staff an opportunity to work together. Gather everyone at the half-way point or at the end of the evening to share highlights and feedback from the calls. Provide food and make it a fun evening!

- **Coordinate individual board thank-you calls.** Many organizations enlist a group of board members to be available to make thank-you calls on an as-needed basis. Create a system with the group so that you can quickly alert them when a gift is received and a call is warranted. E-mail and online sign-up tools such as SignUpGenius.com make coordination of calls easy. Or, if your board members work or live nearby, you can create an index card for each donor who has made a gift, with information on the card about the donor and the gift. Board members can pick up the cards, make the calls on their own time, then return the cards once the calls have been made.

- **Ask board members to write a personal thank-you note.** A thank-you note from a board member is also a meaningful way to thank a donor. To give the note a more personal touch, ask board members to hand-write the notes on personal stationery or a decorative card (rather than signing a typed letter on the organization's stationery).

- **Which donors do you contact?** Of course it would be wonderful to thank everyone with a personal call or note, but that might not be possible. In addition to calling major donors, consider calling first-time donors, donors who have given for several consecutive years, monthly donors, lapsed donors who have recently renewed their giving, and/or donors who have recently increased their gift.

Adapt this form for your board members to use for their thank-you calls to donors.

Sample Phone Call Script

Below is a sample script you can use for your thank-you calls. Please feel free to put this in your own words — it's important that the call is natural, comfortable, and genuine for you.

Hello, is (donor name) at home? Hello, (donor name), my name is _____, I'm a board member of the (your organization) in (your town). I'm not calling to ask you for money. In fact, you made a donation recently of (gift amount) to our organization, and I'm just calling to say thank you!

Stop to let donor respond. If he appears to want to end the call, say:

This is just a quick call to let you know how much your support means to this organization and to (the beneficiaries of your programs and services). Thank you again, and have a good evening.

If donor asks questions, respond as best you can but feel free to say that a staff member would be happy to follow up on any questions. You can also ask one of the following questions:

- *This appears to be a first-time gift for you. I'm always interested to find out how people learned about our work. How did you learn about (your organization)?*

- *I notice you've been giving for several years now. I'm always interested in finding out why people give — I hear such interesting stories. May I ask what has motivated you to give for so many years?*

- *We love to get feedback about our work; it's how we improve. Do you have any comments or suggestions about our work?*

Other items to check with donor:

- *Do we have your correct address?*

- *Do we have your correct e-mail?*

- *How would you prefer to hear updates and news from us?* Check all that apply:

____ Monthly e-newsletter   ____ Volunteer opportunities

____ Special e-mail notices   ____ Personal phone call

____ Personal visit   ____ Annual report

____ Other _____

_____

Adapt this form for board members to use with their thank-you calls.

Donor Information and Call Intake Sheet

Information in box to be completed by development staff prior to call

Name of Donor: _____

Address and E-mail: _____

Phone Number: _____

Giving History: _____

Name of Caller: _____

Was the donor at home? Yes ____   No ____
If not at home, message was left: Yes ____   No ____

Donor Comments:

_____
_____
_____
_____

Questions Donor Asked:

_____
_____
_____
_____

Questions Still Needing Answers or Other Follow-Up Needed:

_____
_____
_____
_____

Other:

_____
_____
_____
_____

ENDNOTES

[i] Edward L. Deci and Richard M. Ryan, pioneers in the field of human motivation, are co-founders of Self-Determination Theory (SDT), a contemporary theory of motivation concerned with supporting one's natural or intrinsic tendencies to behave in effective and healthy ways. SDT has been researched and practiced by a network of researchers from around the world. Deci and Ryan are professors in the Department of Clinical and Social Sciences at the University of Rochester where they direct a pre- and post-doctoral training program focused on SDT. For more, see www.selfdeterminationtheory.org/.

[ii] Burk, Penelope, *The Burk Donor Survey: Where Philanthropy is Headed in 2013*, Cygnus Applied Research, Inc., September 2013, page 49. This 2013 report revealed that 31 percent of donors surveyed who made a gift after receiving a thank-you call from a board member or other top decision maker in the organization attributed the thank-you call to their subsequent decision to give again. And, 27 percent percent of donors surveyed said that they gave a larger gift as a result of having received a thank-you call from a board member or other top decision maker in the organization.

[iii] Bell, Jeanne and Marla Cornelius, *UnderDeveloped: A National Study of Challenges Facing Nonprofit Fundraising*, CompassPoint Nonprofit Services and the Evelyn and Walter Haas, Jr. Fund, San Francisco, CA, 2013. According to the report, development directors' influence on key organizational activities and goals, including financial goals, is uneven. The report says, "Despite the fact that nearly all development directors — 89 percent — serve on management teams, a majority reported only little or moderate influence on the engagement of other staff in fund development or on annual budgeting. High-performing organizations were significantly better on both fronts. 61 percent of development directors in high-performing organizations reported 'a lot of influence' over staff participation in fund development, compared to 41 percent of development directors in the rest of the sample. 66 percent of development directors in high-performing organizations who reported that they have 'a lot of influence' over setting financial goals report that the goals are realistic, compared to 42 percent of development directors in the rest of the sample." In addition, the report found that large numbers of respondents self-assessed the overall effectiveness of their fundraising

activities as either "not at all effective" or only "somewhat effective." The report states that this suggests "that many development directors believe they could be raising much more money if their organizations' leaders would devote more attention and resources to building fundraising capacity and developing a culture of philanthropy."

[iv] Abraham Maslow's theory of the "Hierarchy of Needs" (*Motivation and Personality*, 1954) identifies the need for love and belonging as fundamental and second only to the basic physiological and safety needs such as food, water, shelter, and security. The need for belonging is also central to Adlerian Psychology, which is based on the Viennese psychiatrist Alfred Adler who "emphasized the importance of nurturing feelings of belonging in everyone" (National American Society of Adlerian Psychology, www.alfredadler.org/what-is-an-adlerian). Psychologists Edward Deci and Richard Ryan, co-founders of Self-Determination Theory, cite the need for relatedness or connectedness as one of the three innate psychological needs, along with a sense of autonomy and competence (Deci, Edward, *Why We Do What We Do: Understanding Self-Motivation*, Penguin Group, 1996, p. 88).

[v] Bell, Jeanne and Marla Cornelius, *UnderDeveloped*, p. 15.

[vi] Gottlieb, Hildy, *FriendRaising: Community Engagement Strategies for Boards Who Hate Fundraising but Love Making Friends,* Renaissance Press, 2006, p. 22.

[vii] Axelrod, Terry, *The Benevon Model for Sustainable Funding: A Step-by-Step Guide to Getting it Right*, Benevon Publications, 2012. For more information about the Benevon Model®, see www.benevon.com.

[viii] Badowski, Rosanne with Roger Gittines, *Managing Up: How to Forge an Effective Relationship with Those Above You*, Doubleday, 2003, p. 135.

[ix] Kihlstedt, Andrea, "Train Your Board Members to Ask: Advice From a Board Member and a Trainer" (blog post), *Asking Matters*, April 30, 2013, www.askingmatters.com/blog/train-your-board-members-to-ask-two-perspectives/.

[x] Rabin, Ron, "Blended Learning for Leadership: The CCL Approach" (a white paper published by the Center for Creative Leadership), May 2013, www.ccl.org/leadership/pdf/research/BlendedLearningLeadership.pdf. Note: The 70:20:10 Learning and Development Model was created by Michael M. Lombardo and Robert W. Eichinger, based on research conducted by the Center for Creative Leadership.

xi Nonprofit Research Collaborative. 2012. *Special Report: Engaging Board Members in Fundraising*. Accessed at www.npresearch.org. In this report, the term "signaling" is used to describe the board member's role of indicating the organization's value to the community by his or her own association with the group.

xii Burk, Penelope, *The Burk Donor Survey*.

xiii Ibid.